PROSE & LORE

PROSE & LORE

Issue I
Second Edition

Fall 2012/Winter 2013

EDITOR   Melissa Petro
PUBLISHER   Audacia Ray
COVER & LOGO DESIGN   Shawn Tamaribuchi
INTERIOR DESIGN   Olivia Hall

CONTENTS

INTRODUCTION
Melissa Petro

No matter how our path leads us to it, trading sex defines the people who do it like no other job, trade, occupation, or profession. No matter the complex realities of our experiences, we are thought of as inherently damaged victims, either before or as a result of our profession. Popular representations focus on sex, salacious details, and the potential for sexual exploitation of vulnerable people. They speak over us or for us, assuming we are incapable of speaking for ourselves.

Like most people, as a child I internalized the belief that the life of a sex worker was, if not worthless, worth less. I grew up with no knowledge of the sex industry short of Dateline specials and made-for-TV movies, cautionary tales about girls without families or backstories, girls with fake names like "Candy" or "Mercedes," prostitutes existing only from the waist down. Girls who sold sex were fishnet-stockinged legs leaning into tinted windows idling at red lights. They were girls—never women and certainly never men, and trans women and men were completely invisible. Foolish and desperate, prostitutes and other sex workers were the butt of jokes.

When I became a sex worker, it follows then, I wanted to believe I was exceptional. Raised by my working class, more-or-less single mother, I had clawed my way up from white trashdom to make it to college and, eventually, to New York City where, smart and resourceful, I felt driven to succeed. At the time I sold sex on Craigslist, I was a graduate student at The New School, pursuing a Masters degree in Creative Nonfiction. Thanks to having worked in the sex industry, money was no longer the problem it had been growing up. And yet the money I made in the sex industry was no cure for a growing confusion I felt about myself and my place in the world—confusion that, by twenty-six years old, had become a way of life.

For some, the act of writing is form of social justice, and

writing can be a powerful vehicle for social change. For me, what began as a source of personal healing became my means to enact political change. When I lost my job as a public school teacher for writing about my sex work past, it became my mission to encourage other individuals with minority experiences to inform, engage and inspire audiences by turning their personal experiences into literary nonfiction. I teamed up with the Red Umbrella Project, an organization that does media, storytelling, and advocacy programs by and for individuals with experiences in the sex trades, and we launched The Becoming Writers Workshop, an eight-week memoir writing workshop for people who are currently or formerly involved in the sex trades whether by choice, circumstance, or coercion. In three-hour sessions taught each week in the workshop model, participants read and discussed mentor texts, wrote and shared their work, critiqued one another's writing and engaged in the process of revision. The course culminated with the publication of this anthology and the public performance of the work in it at the Red Umbrella Diaries, a monthly storytelling event that Red Umbrella Project produces in New York City.

The Becoming Writers Workshop, like all Red Umbrella programming, is not just about public storytelling. Our intention was for participants to achieve psychological well-being through personal revelation, and to become better equipped as agents in their own lives and in their community. Ultimately, telling one's own stories increases a person's agency—giving them the strength to understand their circumstances and make choices about their next steps.

Beyond our individual participants, it was our hope that giving people in the sex trades the skills to tell their own stories would have the longer-term effect of reducing stigma attached to people who do transactional sex. If stigma goes down, individuals will have more options and will be better able to provide for themselves and their families.

Today, thanks to writing and performing my work, I see it is no great moral failure to have stripped in college, nor to have had sex for money years later. But the fact that individuals who do so are cast off like trash—not just by serial killers who target sex workers as their victims but in the hearts and minds of the general public—is, in my opinion, what people really ought to feel ashamed of. A great part of overcoming the negative feelings I had associated with my sex work past was learning that I wasn't exceptional, neither before nor as a result of my having sold sex. In the most important ways, I was just like everybody else—just like other people who sold sex and just like people who did not.

Writing and sharing my story helped me to see this—and in serving as Program Coordinator and Instructor of the Becoming Writers Program, I was reminded of this fact. Back in September at the program's start, it was a somewhat humbling experience to read dozens upon dozens of applications from current and former sex workers of all stripes and walks of life, describing their experiences not just as individuals who had worked in the sex trade but as writers, including—for a couple—impressive publication histories. Apparently, I was not the only former sex worker who knew a thing or two about writing! For these individuals, participating in the Becoming Writers Program was an opportunity to amplify their voice and to improve upon the skills they'd already begun developing. Even those students who had never been published and who'd been writing in isolation for years impressed me with their natural talent and the depths of emotional truth they were willing to express. All of our participants, in one way or another, were already writers, and so, in this way, the title of the workshop—Becoming Writers—is a bit of a misnomer.

As a result of the paucity of honest, right-sized representations of sex workers I have felt, at times in my life, a caricature, a figment of other people's imaginations. But I am not—nor are my students, my colleagues, and my friends. We exist, and our writing proves this.

Melissa Petro
December 2012

Kelley Kenney

Notes from the Red Room

I have worked at five body rub studios. The first, in the far west thirties was busted by the cops shortly after its kindly Turkish proprietor was incarcerated for credit card fraud. Thankfully I wasn't at the bust, instead I was toiling at my part-time "straight gig" in optical sales when this happened. I took pride that the second bodywork building stood directly at the midtown east corner where I'd read Dee Dee Ramone and Jim Carroll had hustled in the 70's. I quit that one after a few months when I found myself on a plane to Vegas, instead of present for my shift.

The third was secretly set up in a real office building where bubbly American Indian ladies in charge highly transformed a casting director's workspace with a massage table, candles, and oils. He got free sessions and a small fee in return. I once did an appointment in his waiting room area, giving new meaning to the term "casting couch."

Number four was a rickety one bedroom apartment in the easternmost region of Yorkville, that private pocket of the town seemingly miles from the 6 train. It was run by a 70 something new age lady who was peddling back pain remedies to us on the side. I could tell you so much more about any of these places. But I didn't start taking notes about my clients until I started at place number five, two years ago. I've been there on and off, on when I'm broke, or especially horny. Off when I'm having a sober few months or heavy ethical questions within myself. Or sometimes when I'm just starting to date someone and I can't even handle the thought of being groped by anyone else.

From the lounge of the "massage parlor" where I spent the most time, may I present a smattering of: Notes From the Red Room, Nov 2011-Jan 2012 (insert fanfare here!)

Saturday night, at the end of the night, I saw a consummate hipster. His arms and legs were coated with tattoos; he claimed to be in a band, etc. I weirdly felt like I had something to prove to him, my "coolness." "I live on Bedford," I told him. "Next to El Beit."

"Where do you hang out?" he asked. I don't go out anymore. I don't see bands play, I don't drink. I didn't mention what I do like about the neighborhood, which is the excellent coffee and the good Bikram yoga place. Why AM I living there, I asked myself. To be approved of by the cool kids. I don't need to live in North Brooklyn anymore, I silently realized as I oiled up my hands.

He was having trouble staying hard, not my fault. I was sweating from my 110% bodily effort. He kept moving around, more than practically any dude I'd had on that bed before—oh, all the men, all of their flanks and thighs and heft and sadness and needs; their bodies stretched across the cheap sheets, waiting for me. Like that line from *Jesus Christ Superstar*, "I've had so many men before/in very many ways/he's just one more." Oh, the weight. Yeah, yeah, yeah.

"You're gonna make the mattress fall off!" I scolded.

He apologized sheepishly, still squirming. "I'm such a wiggle worm," he said, "I don't know what the problem is." Maybe you shouldn't have immediately mentioned spending the day with your wife and your son, twice. Maybe you could have removed your wedding band. It still bugs me when they leave them on. How do I know which relationships have, you know, "understandings" (some do! I think...), and which are being thwarted? I know it has nothing to do with me, but I do NOT get turned on feeling, to paraphrase Slick Rick, a wedding band on THIS bitch's ass cheek. It's not a client's job to make me feel comfortable, and in some cases I'm sure it's a transgressive thrill to see my labia reflected in one's precious metal, but EW. Maybe to remove the ring is to make oneself aware that one is removing it.

I had one session yesterday, at 5:30. He was a Clark Kent: bespectacled banker dude to the outside world; pocket Lothario in the Red Room. "Feel that big hard cock," he instructed me. "Is this cock big enough for ya?" I looked at it. It was certainly medium-sized, and not skinny. I wasn't sure if it had been a rhetorical question, like when people say "hot enough for ya?" or if he expected a thought-out response. I was momentarily confused, looking at his wielded appendage. "Yes," I replied, with certainty. It was big enough for me. I dared myself to touch his wedding ring in a way he would notice, thinking about what I wrote yesterday. Doing so was like licking a frozen flagpole, or touching Boo Radley's house. A dare. I hoped I didn't smear lube on it. That silicone stuff can be such a bitch to clean off.

I had this Canadian guy recently. "Do you do role-playing?" he asked.

"Yes. What kind?" I asked.

"You know... I hear you're an actress..." he began.

"I'm NOT!" I interrupted. I'm not. The manager

ALWAYS tells guys that on the phone, as if to increase my value: you're not lining the lazy pocket of a gal who kind of, sort of, thinks-slash-fears she's incapable of doing any other kind of work—you're Helping a Starving Artist! Your contribution of $200 and a palmful of your semen, while not tax-deductible, will directly assist in the accomplishment of a young (always, always seven-to-eight years less than the truth. If they guess anything closer, even 26, it feels like a betrayal) woman's bohemian dreams! You're a philanthropist, not a philanderer! Nothing selfish about YOU sir, no sir! "Captain Save-a-Ho," Kristen, a lady who was working here when I first started, called it.

Big sigh from yours truly. "What KIND of role-play?" I repeated. (Actually I LOVE doing role-play, being a supervillainess or inappropriate boss-lady or something, but not in this context. They're for BDSM sessions, when one's mind is primed to focus for an hour, at least in my opinion. Time spent here in the rooms of the body rub studio are intended for personal mental zen-ness, and I prefer to conduct it nearly silent.)

"I don't know," he responded, "just talk to me."

Another sigh here. I am so bad at talking dirty on command. It's embarrassing. I really dislike saying the word "pussy," for example, even for money. You can see it; I'll show it to you. You can touch it, sure (wait, did you wash your hands? The city is dirty. You may have touched a subway pole recently. Hang on, let me just grab a baby wipe for you. Paws out, please. There, that's better. Okay, proceed!). I just don't want to call it anything, okay? Perhaps I come from the "show, don't tell" school of sex work. Also, there are different concepts of what "dirty talk" is. If I must, I need a conversation, not a monologue. If a client requests a steady stream of heavy humiliation, after awhile I just run out of things to say. There are only so many word combinations for, like, "you maggoty little particle of pig shit. You little cock-guzzling slut machine," or whatever, before your mouth gets tired and it's boring as hell.

He was doing Things to my Parts with his hand, and he said something in Canadianese (about his penis, uncreatively self-described as "big, hard") and I laughed. I couldn't help it—sometimes Canadian men sound like Valley Girl teens, with an upward lilt to the end of their phrases. Maybe I felt instantly trapped in some lost *Kids in the Hall* sketch. "That's not supposed to be funny!" he said. But it was!

I am reading Secret Diary of a Call Girl. I am envious because (a) it's published (b) I'm getting a, "is this woman a bigger perv than me?" feeling. When did it become a contest, dear, I ask myself. What would the prize be? A gilded toilet to drink from? Kinkiness isn't the Olympics.

I had five of the eight total sessions on Monday. It feels good to occasionally get to be the star of the house.

Monday... Two hours with this guy we'd both forgotten I'd seen before, with glasses made of wood—that's how I eventually remembered him, from the glasses. He kept saying quietly, "what?" during the whole session, as in, what am I thinking. I dislike that question the most. Just ask me where I'm from originally, or the dreaded "what do you do when you're not here?" or the worse-worded, "what do you want to be when you grow up?" I answer truthfully but curtly, not feeling the need to create a false backstory for myself, but not really wanting a client to imagine me dancing/singing/watching TV on my couch/writing (about them)/visiting my hometown in upstate New York.

My thoughts are my last layer of private property, and you want me to give that up, too? "You want to know what I'm actually thinking?" I said. "I'm thinking about how you look like a priest from the church I went to growing up." He actually looked like two of them, Fathers Dominic and Bob, middle-aged and heavyset, but well-groomed. Thick-browed and dark-haired, with kind eyes. Italian-American. I really told him this, not caring about his reaction, if he would be put off, or turned on. He wanted to know what I was thinking. He didn't respond, reached for his suddenly-vibrating phone to take a work call. I crouched by his calves at the foot of the bed, pleased to have to be quiet for a few minutes, moving us closer to the end of the two hours he'd booked. I usually end sessions early. I think forty minutes is plenty for an hour. In therapy you only get forty-five, and no orgasm (presumably).

Who else did I see? It's scary how you forget.

Yesterday: Friday. I saw this new guy who was short and had been to one of the dungeons where I'd worked, and I gave him my number for future sessions. I used this strawberry lube in my mouth, from the supply basket on the bedside table. "Do you usually use this stuff?" he asked. No, just doing an experiment. And it worked! It actually tasted pretty good.

Second was a young guy named Will with a tattoo of a bird on his stomach that said, "music is salvation," which reminded me of banners at churches. He was super respectful but didn't smell that great.

Third was Dave of Texas, so tan. I vaguely remembered him, but he remembered me. "I saw you six months ago, and I can remember what we were listening to," he said. "Jane's Addiction." Yup. Last May/June I was crazy about the Red Room mixed with track number six on *Ritual de lo Habitual*: "Three Days." "What do I get for remembering?" he asked. "Um... this," I said, and licked his balls.

I was bleeding but hoped he wouldn't notice. I do this sometimes; a game I personally call, I have my period, let's see if I can hide it! A darkish room and quick condom removal (make it seem like you're just really nice and thorough, and use baby wipes to take it off) and even quicker moving of towels to cover any spots on the bed take care of this- though more than once I then saw smears on the pillowcase. Dirty! I love it. I want to not, like, ruby-shower heavy bleed on someone, but reach inside myself with a couple fingers and write my name on a dude's chest with it. C-h-l-o-e. Smiley face. I will always remember that time in 2001 in South Carolina or wherever that was, with Shawn, when we got bloody handprints on the hotel wall, and we left it looking like a crime scene. Oh, that's why they call period sex "crime-scene sex," I remember thinking, though I only heard it called that once.

I watch myself in the mirrors at work constantly. It makes it more interesting. I used to do this ages ago out of worry of my body not looking right. Now I'm curious about what my "work moves" look like, my whiteness with a slash of dark lace underwear, my tattoos (my "permanent epaulets") in contrast, in profile, my back arching doing a downward dog over the guy's back before I slide down it, serpentine chin first to rub my cheek against his neck. I think about sex all the time because it's my job. I want to make room for other stuff. I want to think about other stuff. I think?

I watch my limbs intertwine with what are often substantially darker ones supine below me. On the curtained bed in the red-walled, chandeliered room I make a burlesque of a bordello with my music selections (for example, the soundtrack to *Flashdance*). I look sexy indeed but it's strange to watch because it's really just a long-ago choreographed dance, every time with a different partner. There are slightly different turns and dips, but I can almost do the counts. I feel unfair for offering this processed sex. They don't care. Maybe I am good enough of an actress, or good enough of an empathy to make it seem authentic. Sometimes it feels that way. Sometimes they catch me watching myself bend and writhe. They usually watch. I watch myself kissing them out of the corner of my eye, to see what it looks like.

Last night he and I were sitting on the floor of his room back in Brooklyn with a mirror to my left, talking about mirrors. Ceiling mirrors, wall mirrors, how I have five mirrors in my bedroom, how I would like a room of all mirrors, with curtains you can pull over them all like in a dance studio. I scooched forward in my jeans. I'm wearing jeans, I pointed out, because I hardly ever wear jeans. We kissed and kissed and I carefully avoided his giant still-wet brand-new tattoo. I looked up over his shoulder into the mirror, and there was my little face, and me fully clothed. This is what I look like kissing someone for real, I thought, and looked for a second but then stopped because it felt weird.

Kelley Kenney is the nom de plume of a writer and off-and-on sex worker living in New York. This is her first publication, although she's been keeping journals privately for over twenty years.

Aimee Herman

The first time I was afraid of my life was the first time I felt alive

It was awkward like the first day of school or trying to eat ribs without getting the sauce beneath my fingernails. While she pressed her mass on top of me, I counted the stars or were they airplanes? They flirted, blinking their silver lights. Then she inserted her finger and I worried her nail polish might flake inside me, creating an infection. Then a moan and was that mine? August is the perfect month to lose one's virginity because the night air is so dismissive to the sweat sweetly intoxicating fast-moving parts and although the mosquitoes tempted us with suggestions of an orgy, it was just us beneath the plastic swing-set held captive in her parent's backyard. At first, I could only focus on the scent of Parliament cigarettes on her skin. It was too dark to create pictures connected by her freckles but I could feel them grind into me. Another finger and the mosquitoes have ignored our request for solitude and what if one bites me on my vagina? She kisses me with a tongue that feels monstrous, but warm and tastes of what I imagine I must taste like and she doesn't really want me to touch her and I worry she's just pretending I'm her boyfriend or our boss whose suits always drag against the movie theatre tile. The moon is watching and it's kind of like a giant nightlight guiding our limbs. Her fist is inside me and this is love, right? Is this love?

Light sensitive daguerreotypes and the warning of corrosion

I need to tell you that things are going to change. I need to tell you that your hair will get brighter; your habits will grow more expensive and disruptive; your reason for coming to Brooklyn will become replaced by poor decisions. I need to tell you that you are going to fall, literally. You are going to sit in a movie theatre next to a woman who you think you are in love with. Then, you will head to your favorite lesbian bar, which will close down two years after you fall in front of it. You will walk inside and she will order you a pint of something locally brewed. You won't feel right. You will tell her you need to walk outside for some air. You will feel dizzy and panicked. This is the moment you fall, face parallel to the concrete. You won't remember calling out her name as your chin, opened up and bloody, frightens everyone that stands above you as spectators. You will wait in the ER for over an hour, forego plastic surgery on your chin to save time, and receive nine stitches. You will spend the next two weeks trying to convince everyone that your fall had nothing to do with being drunk (you hadn't taken a sip yet). You will explain that you got lost inside a moment of panic. You won't explain that it had to do with your mother trying to commit suicide again (yes, she does it again and you will admit her to New York Methodist for ease and convenience) and the stress of lying about how you make your money (I'm not sure you are ready to hear that part yet). Because of this fall, you will have to go to the dentist. This will cost a lot because you have no insurance. You will have to go to the dentist because you will notice with your tongue that your tooth is cracked and when you are bored, you will reach your fingers far back there and try pulling it out. Suddenly, you will have a piece of your tooth in your palm and then you will become obsessed with running your tongue over the remaining part. It is rigid and sharp. You will start to worry that more things are wrong in your mouth, so you finally make an appointment. When you get there, you will explain your fear of dentists, doctors and anyone trying to inspect your body. The dentist is a woman; this makes things easier. However, she will tell you that you need a root canal. This procedure is extremely painful and expensive. It will take you a year to pay off that bill. I need to tell you that you are going to receive text messages from your dealer. (Yes, you relapse). He is going to contact you on your birthday, when you are doing your best to stay out of trouble by attending an open mic so you can read your poetry. He is going to ask for a blow job in exchange for free coke. You are going to consider this. (I'm not sure you are ready to hear why). You will ignore him this time. You are going to try to kill yourself on New Year's Eve two months before you turn 26. It will snow. You will be staying at your sister's house while she is away. You will have a lot of coke, hoarded and saved. You will order Chinese food. You will watch two Woody Allen movies. You will write a note to your family that you later rip up because writing a suicide note will seem too romantic and narcissistic. You will finish all the coke and cut yourself. You will wake up the next morning with a sore nose, cracked and red, with dried blood all over your arms. You will tell no one of this. I need to tell you that things are going to change. You will buy a box of condoms but never open the box. You will start obsessing over sexually transmitted diseases and pregnancy. You will take more showers. You will memorize the scent of semen. Are you ready for this? Are you sure? You will become a sex worker. You will grow into a seasoned liar. You will gather most of your income from giving middle-aged white men (which you later refer to as MAWMs) foot jobs then blow jobs then offering up your homosexual vagina for cash. You will meet many men and fuck them for money, which you will save up in a white, business sized envelope that you hide in a cigar box that you purchase for two dollars at a stoop sale. You will use a lot of this money on aforementioned relapse. However, you will still save up enough to make a move to Colorado. I know this is unexpected. I know the idea of leaving New York seems tragic. You will impulsively apply to a writing program at a university to finally finish your bachelor's degree. You will get in. You will feel like this is a sign to remove yourself from the trauma you created in Brooklyn. You will use all the saved up twenties stacked up neatly in white envelope and this will get you there. You will clean yourself up, staying away from drugs for almost seven months; then, you will relapse again in Colorado. You will find yourself working once again as a sex worker. You will expand from bedrooms to parking garages to hotel rooms to offices. I need to tell you that things will never be the same. Your body will never recover. You will become diagnosed with HPV. You will fall in love with the best woman you've ever breathed against. You will tell her what you've done. You will worry you passed your disease onto her. You will find relief when her tests come out negative. She will clean you up. Unfortunately, you will lose her too. Perhaps you shouldn't be reading this. Perhaps this is too much to fathom. Perhaps there is no such thing as warnings, only condolences.

Fifth floor drive-through

The air is slippery. There is a thick aroma of pollution collapsed into my hair. I am waiting for his RAV4 to pull up to this fifth floor office called parking garage. I can hear the sounds of lunch breaks down below. Tire wheels. The slam of cigarettes thrown out of half-open windows. I am wearing my favorite jeans—the only pair that fit me right—and a loose button-down gauzy shirt that reveals my black lace bra. I will leave all my clothes on; this one only wants my mouth. He is twelve minutes late and the clock is running. I search for a pattern within the license plates—they are all Colorado. I notice the bad taste in my mouth, which will only get worse once his dick is in there. It is dark in my office. There are no posters, nor is there a coffee machine or water cooler. No one sweeps these floors. No one cares enough to notice the gum wrappers and cigarette carcasses. I leave my car on to hear the music playing. I choose a station to put my mouth in the mood.

Performance poet Aimee Herman was recently featured at the LGBT Fresh Fruit Festival. She sews limbs on words to see how far they can stretch. Her work can be read in dead (g)end(er), THRUSH, *and* Lavender Review. *She's a former sex worker and current sex activist. Aimee edits erotica for* Oysters & Chocolate *and is a host for the Inspired Word performance series. Find her writing poems on her body in Brooklyn or at aimeeherman.wordpress.com.*

Dominick

Vitis Vinifera 'Fantasy'

I haven't had anything to eat except the Clif Bar I'd stuck in my back pocket. It had been steamrollered nearly flat by my ass, and was now something like fruit leather, except with crunchy bits. What they provide in the Tombs is barely fit for human consumption: a sandwich of stale white bread (how does bread so processed and preserved even go stale?) and a stingy smear of something they call "p'nut-butta'an-jelly" but is some pre-combined sludge bearing no resemblance to, nor containing, either, or both.

After thirty-six hours of lock-up and a court appearance, I am released to the wilds of Lower Manhattan. I approach a pushcart fruit vendor with a few dollars left in my front pocket and make impulsive, not very sensible selections. Rather than wait to get into the bag and peel and wash something, I take one grape off the stem, and make a pleading gesture with my eyes at the vendor. She accedes, and I put the dusty, almost black globe in my mouth. It is warmish from sitting out on the shaded cart on a steamy summer morning. Its juice is syrupy and biting. Its viscous flesh is rushing my tongue and invading my palate with the lush miracle of the plant kingdom and the bounty of the soil and it is my salvation and my freedom and my delicious.

Cali Boy

He's new to the city, running from his lab-concocted demon, breaking out of the shuttered nihilism of addiction. He's run right into my quirky home group, the bright-eyed stalwarts of recovery. During fellowship at a Polish diner, he throws out a request for a couch to sleep on for a few nights, and I offer mine. It's an agenda-free courtesy to a young man with good intentions. He's not my type particularly. I've always favored the swarthy, the olive-complected, the caramel, the dusky, the brown-skinned. He's a California boy, dirty blond with blue eyes. Although he is tall and lanky, and that is a build I favor.

I hadn't noted the depths of his withdrawal; he was good at covering. Now that we're in close quarters, it's evident he's got a bad case of the shakes. He twitches all up and down his long limbs. His skin is marred by scratched-open sores—they seem regularly spaced, like a polka-dot fabric with a large repeat. We tell each other our stories and tease out our dreams while lying on my bed, away from the blathering television in the living room. Exile to the couch seems out of the question. We fortify my bedroom against the demon: blinds are drawn, talismans are carefully positioned (bottle caps, dice, driftwood, river stones), we are cocooned in blankets, and the cat is on guard at the foot of the bed. I hold him on those crisp fall nights to allay the twitching and the scratching. His body temperature runs high and steady, like a wood-burning oven after its cast-iron body has absorbed the big flames, throwing off the heat of bright embers. After a few restless nights, the shakes subside and he settles in my embrace.

Our mutual attraction makes itself known during our overnight clutches—our breathing deepens, our hearts pulse harder, stiff cocks press into soft parts. I begin to discern his scent as the demon residue slicks out of his body. But nothing more will come of this intimacy, I tell myself; it would be a breech and a complication. Besides, he's not my type particularly, right? My resolve lasts less than a week. Embracing every night, we've been holding each other and holding back. In an instant, as last grains fall through the hourglass neck, our embrace goes from taut to fluid, I rub my limbs along his, I caress his thighs and his shoulders and the small of his back. I nuzzle into his neck, inhale, and draw his essence into me.

My Cali boy holds the demon at bay—the sores heal, his body temperature drops a bit, and we emerge a public entity, a relationship. We bond over late nights playing games and watching movies—optimistic fare with songs and beautiful people. We coax out more revelations. We struggle to define our respective roles, and to support the good habits we're both chasing—clean living, simple kindness. "Let's just be honest no matter what, and let's not ever go to sleep angry, okay?" and he's earnest and I agree and I mean it. The giddiness of new romance outshines any struggle, until the road twists and the demon rears its head.

Meth is deliberate and persistent and potent and stimulating and euphoria-inducing, and the demon seeps under the front door, now between the blinds, and knocks over the talismans and scares the cat. A sparkling pile melts into wafts of smoke in the bulbous end of a glass pipe, you inhale a pretty waft, then spit out skin and teeth and lung tissue and receptors and tainted essence, which slicks into the soil and causes superfund sites. The sores rage anew, same polka dot pattern, just shifted over; he's scratching them open again. Now suspicion clouds my every sky.

During a visit to California, a roaring freeway growls between us. We retreat to a desert oasis and stay with one of his many older male "friends." One cool desert night, he leaves our bed. I awake in the middle of the night for a pee and hear their moans through the master bedroom doors. It's an unforgivable betrayal, mainly because I had to listen to it. "I couldn't sleep… we were just talking… it just sorta happened," and this is uncomfortably close to how our own relationship developed. Duffel bag on my back, I walk miles through the desert dawn, and make my way home to our shattered fortress, aggrieved, dumbstruck. Sometimes you have to walk away.

Only some months later, after seeing a change in his relationship status on Facebook, does the loss register, and it is pure loss, and I am ransacked. It stings and it burns and it gives me a steady seize of panic. I fall into a deep, monotonous despair. I lost him, my twitchy, hot-running, gangly body all knees and elbows, hapless homebody, computer nerd, talisman collector, game-playing geek boy, with skin redolent of skate parks and sugar and dew. My not-particularly-my-type Cali boy's bright, unsteady blue eyes are now reflecting some crooked man's light two thousand, eight hundred and twenty-seven miles away. I would walk for one thousand hours—hike mountain passes, cross plains, cut through forests, and trudge through   deserts—for   a   fix.

A Dialog, Gouverneur Street, NYC

"Well Rocco always takes my checks."

"Well 'Rocco' isn't here, is he? And he didn't say anything about checks to me."

I was beginning to doubt Rocco's very existence. He had set me up on this call online. It was supposed to be a three-hour tag team, and that's good money. The john is into fisting and enjoys guys with large hands and muscles. Shortly after I arrive, the john got a phone call.

"Rocco's been in a taxicab accident and won't be coming."

Oh. I go through with the call anyway, despite my suspicions. The john instructs me to apply the coke to his asshole, then insert my hand, and turn it slowly, like we are some kind of clock mechanism, but made of flesh instead of precision steel. His proclivity for this sensation of a measured rotation of the hand is how he came up with his online handle: "Revolutions." Ok, whatever, butt puppet. I strain to make eye contact with him, peering over his fat rolls as he hoists his ass up high off of his kitchen table. My hand, slathered in veterinary lubricant, is buried in his rectum, and his hole is gaping and bloody from all the coke and the workout.

It's long past time to wrap up this sordid call, and I feel that the whole scene is unraveling. Have I been taken in by a scheming, manipulative, morbidly obese, coked-out fisting bottom? With a rubber checkbook where a stack of bills should be?

"Get dressed," I say as I gather up his wallet and his three vials of coke, "We're going to the ATM."

"Dominick" is a Brooklyn-born Italian who spent his twenties as a kept boy. In the wake of his Sugar Daddy's alcohol-related death, he was left a modest fortune that fueled his own addiction. He started escorting in recovery to reclaim sex work on his own terms, retiring after three years to take a management position in commercial real

estate. Dominick now writes for blog.rentboy.com, offering escorts and clients alike advice drawn from his experience. He's a frequent presence at Red Umbrella Diaries, and has appeared in Dan Savage's podcast and "Savage Love" column. He'll appear in the upcoming anthology Johns, Marks, Tricks & Chickenhawks, *published by Soft Skull Press.*

Essence Revealed

Push and Pull

Essence: the intrinsic nature of indispensable quality of something, especially something abstract that determines its character.

"Do you need encouragement to get out of the house or support to stay home?"

Chad was trying to decipher what I needed through my tears.

"I have to go to work," I sobbed. "I haven't been able to make myself go and bills are due."

Chad had been my confidant for years, ever since I'd met him at a regular bar where I'd once tried to get a job. I was told by an employee that the boss loved black women and that they were looking for bartenders. Yet, when I went in, I was given what I've come to learn is the, "we won't just say to you that we don't hire black bartenders" run around. They told me three different times to come back. The manager wouldn't even come out to speak to me. Apparently, his boss must only love to fuck black women like me in private, not hire them in plain daylight.

Sitting at the bar that third time, I realized no one behind the bar was a person of color. The "Currently Hiring Bartenders" sign was still in the window. I would have to stick with the stripping job.

At least I met Chad.

"OK," Chad was saying, "you know you're beautiful, talented, and smart. You have a great body—especially those abs—and that cute butt. You're kind and one of the most industrious people I know. Call me when you get to your car and I will pump you up with some more good karma."

Somehow, if anyone else had said these kinds of things to me when I was feeling down, my reaction would've been nothing but an eye roll. Knowing Chad was with me managed to get me to pick myself up off of the kitchen floor and peel my back away from the cabinets. Someone earlier in the week had told me that they could see the sadness dripping off of me. I felt like it had dripped off of me abundantly enough to create a pool of sadness chin deep. That day, Chad was the floatation device I needed to swim out of it.

He spoke to me as I drove into work, cracking corny yet funny jokes. He was always so cheery. Sometimes it made me nauseous how chipper he always was. On days like this I was deeply grateful for him.

Finally, I got to the club. "I'll be up until about 11 p.m. if you need another dose of good karma," he said right before he hung up.

All I could think was, God bless you. All I said was, "Thank you."

Point of view: the perspective from which a story is told. In acting, a term used to describe the cover given the true meaning behind the words. For example, the soap opera star may say, "I'm great!" with a big smile. But as the audience we know the truth because we just saw a scene where he was weeping over his mother's grave.

I walk into the strip club to start my shift feeling like a wilted flower. I pass a group of dancers on my way to the dressing room. One of them jokingly shouts, "Oh, great, she's here." I shoot a sarcastic smile, "Oh, please." While I get dressed, my face is blank. I turn me off and focus on turning my stripper persona on. What is my earning goal for the night? How close am I to my earning goal for the week? How many dances and/or VIP Room sales does that equate to? I have to leave my personal shit at the door. I have to remember the reason that I'm here. I have to remember what the service that I am providing is all about. The customers want to feel appreciated and attractive.

Thongs, gown, heels, hair, make-up, last looks, and head out onto the floor with a HUGE SMILE. I walk the floor introducing myself to everyone I pass as I make my way to the DJ booth to check in and then to pay my house fee. I don't try to get any money from the men yet. I just say a friendly hello. On my way back, on the floor, I get stopped to do a few dances from someone I had introduced myself to. Afterwards, I go sit at the bar so that I can watch the room for any good customers, have a drink and wait for my first set on stage.

While I'm sitting at the bar another dancer, Arielle, approaches me. She is a honey brown, light skin black woman with big, curly hair.

"Can I ask you a question?" she says.

"Sure."

"How do you do what you do?" she asks me. "How do you always make money?"

"HA! Well, A, I don't always make money but I never show that I'm upset when I'm here. B, I focus on selling when I am here. I talk to everyone that I can. C, I bring them the sunshine. They come in here to escape from the real world of being husband, boss, dad, whatever."

"Ugh, I can't stand even talking to them."

"Yeah, they probably can tell. You gotta make them

think that you sincerely find them fascinating and are interested."

My name is called and I get up to go onstage. I dance and smile at every guy that makes eye contact with me like he is the only one in the room. My goal is to make them feel like I think they are the only one in the club. While I'm up there, I feel out who I should go over to right when I get off the stage. Who seems to think that we have a "special" connection? That is who I will go and have a drink with. While he is ordering the drink, I excuse myself for a second so that I can go say thanks to any guys who tipped me onstage. If they want a dance I promise that I'll come over after I finish my drink. I line them up. "Oh, sweetie, I have two guys ahead of you but I'm coming right over after that."

All night, I'm the flirty life of the party. I smile, dance with wild abandon, crack naughty jokes and cling to their every word. Once four a.m. arrives, I can turn it all off. I wipe off the make-up. I put on the baggy sweats I wore there. I stuff my money roll in my sock and I drive home. I watch late night/early morning TV silliness until I decompress enough to fall asleep.

Push

Before my eyes even open, I can feel my stomach churning as I wake up. It is that familiar dread of having to live through another day. I haven't gone to work in a week and I don't care. I lie here in bed not seeing a reason to get up. I'm not hungry, so I don't eat. I don't have any auditions. I don't have to be anywhere. I can't come up with any reason to move from this very spot… ever. I may know a good amount of people but I have very few friends. No one will check up on me or know that I've been laying here for a week.

I'm pissed off every time I have to go to the bathroom. It's the only action I begrudgingly take. I haven't bathed all week either. Why bother? It's just me, myself and I here and I won't offend me. When I do have to leave for an audition, I grab whatever clothing matches from the pile of clothes on the floors at the side of my bed. My apartment is dark but my eyes have adjusted enough to pick through the pile when I have to leave the house for an audition. That's the only reason to go outside by my estimation. No one in there will know what I'm going through. They don't care. Leave your shit at the door, show up on time, and be professional. I've perfected this public presentation.

There is a light wood wardrobe to one side of my bed. Staring at the pattern takes up the bulk of my days. The other parts of the day are spent looking at the eggshell white wall to the other side of my bed. This wall has a framed black and white picture of a black woman lying on her stomach with her round behind peeking out from under the sheets. Sometimes tears will stream down my eyes. My facial muscles can't be bothered to participate in these crying games.

Pull

I'm sitting in a waiting room at an audition, a group of blacktresses are talking about how slow business has gotten.

"Remember when we used to go out three and four time a day?"

"Girl, yes! If I get out three times a week, that's good."

"Three times a week!? This is my first appointment in three weeks."

Everyone mmmhmm's and aha's about the situation. Eventually, the conversation rolls around to what we are going to do to make a living now.

"I started working at TVI studios. Hopefully, meeting some of these TV/Film casting directors will parlay itself into some work."

"Chile, I had to go back to the restaurant. Lawd knows I didn't want to but I gotta pay rent."

"My husband just looks at anything I make as extra money. He said as far as him setting up the household budget is concerned, I'm unemployed."

We all start to laugh at that. I feel slightly jealous that she has a partner that supports her and her art. Only slightly, though, because she has three kids to raise and I don't want to do that! This entire time, I've been quiet. I find that when I'm quiet people tend not to notice. They are usually too busy talking about themselves to care that I'm not. I look at my roller bag. I know that inside of it are seven-and-a-half-inch clear stilettos, several different colored thongs and long gowns, baby wipes, and bags of make-up. I had finally escaped from the clutches of my bed enough to get to work.

It's Tuesday so that means that Steve will be coming in tonight. He comes in between midnight and one a.m. to the strip club. He comes in that late hoping I'll be done with any other customers. He wants to get me to himself. He usually gets me all to himself. He's wearing khakis and a polo shirt. He's a middle aged, balding white man. He's a truck driver. He's pretty fun to be around.

If I'm on stage when he comes in, he'll have my drink waiting for me. He usually sits near the waitress station at the bar. I'll sip on the Malibu and pineapple juice he ordered for me while we chit-chat about everything and nothing. His daughter and her skills as an artist are his latest proud dad fodder for conversation. If I dare mention that he should buy a dance or go to the VIP room, he'll protest. If I just sit and talk with him for a bit, he'll eventually want to go into the VIP room for an hour. Once we are up there he takes off his polo shirt and khakis. He's still fully dressed. Underneath he wears leggings, knee high boots, a lady's shirt and bra stuffed with the chicken cutlet looking breast enhancers with pearl shaped earring stuck in them to create the nipple effect. Now, I call him Stephanie.

"Man, I went to this cross dresser party and all these gay guys were trying to hit on me. It was awful."

"I'm sorry, Stephanie…"

"Where can a guy wearing a dress go to meet straight women?"

"I don't know, but this is New York so it must happen somewhere around here."

Every time the VIP hostess comes up to let us know that our hour is over, he pays to stay another hour. We are having a great time. We make up stories about all the adventures we'd have walking hand in hand in Amsterdam. In between talking and laughing, I dance for him. Sadly, the club has to close and he has to go home and be Steve.

Push

It's Thursday which means Count Dracula is my regular customer tonight. He earned the name from the chocolate dancers he has a fancy for. I suppose we could have named him Count Chocula. He has a thick German accent, greasy grey hair and smells like he hasn't bathed or brushed his teeth… ever. The smell of red wine and cigarettes permeate his breath. However, he will want to stay in the VIP room for two, three, four hours, which means one thousand, fifteen hundred, two thousand dollars.

He whispers way too closely to my nose. "You have three lahverz unt one of dem iz a vooman. You ahr such an ahrtizan, so soft, so tender."

I get up to escape the smell of his breath and start to dance for him, facing away from him. As I hover over his lap, he trips me up so that I land on his lap. He grabs my arms, "You run but da chase, da chase, eet eet iz all a parht of eet izint it?" I try to get up but I can't. "You need sumwan who will be dere for you… help you out financially frum time to time... someone who will not restrict your movement." He has me pinned down by my arms. I sigh as I sit and listen. I regulate my breath so that I am breathing out in order to avoid breathing in that smell of his. Then his hand starts to make its way to my thong. I forcefully free one arm so that I can grab his hand before it reaches my pussy. "Don't move, leave it, leave it, I vant you to enjoy it." HOW could he possibly think that this is enjoyable for me? I use Jiu-Jitsu-like moves to keep his prying hand away.

He is what we call in the industry "a lot of work." We tend to rotate him among us because some weeks, ya just don't have the mental energy for the fight. I keep checking the time on my watch every so often behind his head. I close my eyes and picture twenty one-hundred-dollar bills to help ease the time on by. I think about how many people say stripping is easy money. I daydream about punching someone in the mouth next time I hear those words escape from their lips.

Pull

It's Friday and a group of high rollers have come in for a bachelor party. There are about ten of them. They have corralled about twenty strippers to party with them in the far back right corner of the club. It is one of Tommy's last few nights of "freedom." They celebrate by popping bottle after bottle of champagne. They were making it "rain" on us with one-hundred-dollar stacks of singles at a time. We were given garbage bags to collect our money. What they were spending had long since gone over the limits of what we could fit into our purses. In the dressing room there is a house mom. She keeps an eye on things in the dressing room and sells to or provides us with anything we could possibly need from aspirin and tampons to dresses and shoes. Those of us who were close with her handed her our bags of money for her to organize while we headed back out to make more. She got big tips that night.

There is an electric energy in that corner of the room: the music, the pace, bottle after bottle of Cristal popping, the rush of extreme celebration. Tonight, I forget to remember that I'm supposed to be ashamed. I forget to remember how much I'm supposed to hate this game. I'm getting paid to hang out and play. This is a mutually beneficial fantasy. They get to be that player that knows how to keep the "dime pieces" running his way. I get to be that "I deserve every bit of money in your pocket just cuz I look like me" kinda chick. THIS is an excellent night at the night job.

Push

I'm sad. Not just "it'll pass in a little while" sad. I'm "been spending all my free time alone for the last few months constantly on the brink of tears" sad. I'm "sit on the side of the building sobbing uncontrollably as New York ignores me and gets on with its day" sad. I'm "sit on the subway and let the tears freely flow down my apathetic face" sad. I'm "so numb that I can't even muster my usual doses of hope and positivity" sad.

I thought I did everything right. I stayed in school. I stayed out of trouble. I got amazing grades which led to an over priced education at a big name school. I graduated cum laude. I followed my passion and did what I loved. I even ate my vegetables. So, I cannot comfortably grasp why I am not able to figure out another way to take care of myself besides stripping.

Stripping itself isn't the problem. It's a job with pros and cons like any other job. I love being able to work as little or as much as I choose. I love that how much I make is on me. The more I develop my sales skills by studying sales books, the better I become at selling VIP rooms. The biggest thing that can stop me is me and my moods. The main thing that makes this seem like a sucky way to make a living is the negative outside perception. This stigmatized perception affects how I am treated by some customers at work. It definitely affects how I am treated by anyone outside of work that is able to pin the label stripper on me.

My eyes open one morning and I look up to see depression over me. It has me by the neck. I wish I would just disappear so that I can finally be released from its clutches. My kind of depression, though, isn't the kind that is strong and willful enough to make me harm myself. It just buzzes annoyingly and incessantly like a fly. It is only strong enough to make me not see the point in... anything, everything.

Pull

I have to get out of New York for a while. Maybe a change of environment will put me in better spirits. I research what I will need to go work in Vegas. This is another benefit of this job. I can go to just about any major city in the world and find work. I have to get a business license to work in Vegas. I read online that ladies will get employment paperwork from a club that they don't want to work at but will be easily hired for. I also have to get fingerprints done. It is suggested that I get to the fingerprinting office early to avoid the long lines. I find an extended stay hotel that looks like a mini apartment for a really reasonable rate. It's near the club that is my first choice. I book it for two weeks. I got most of this information by lurking around on stripperweb.com.

When I land in Vegas it is too late to do fingerprints. I find a dinky club to audition for. Why is this club so dark? The manager might as well be a part of the anti-marketing campaign for this spot. "You'll make more money working some place else. Oh, and you have to wear two thongs at all times when you're working." I have never heard this rule before or since. My imagination runs wild with reason and scenarios that could have brought this rule to be. Do the customers here have some kind of stealth thong penetrating skills or something? Are two thongs like kryptonite to their thong-penetrating super powers? Employment paperwork in hand, I walk out of this dive forever. I got what I needed which is the paperwork to get my business license in the morning.

Business license in hand and fingerprints done. The first club I went to wouldn't even let me audition. I look around and I don't see any women of color working. It must be one of those clubs that is a land of a million blondes. They probably have about three black women on the entire roster. They claim that it is because the clientele is not interested in women of color. Yet, I make my money from mainly and almost primarily white men. It's annoying, insulting, and belittling. Next, I go to Spearmint Rhino. The manager leads me to the dressing room to get changed. It's about the size of an entire club in New York. There's tons of counter space with mirrors that have light bulbs going across the top. There are so many dancers buzzing in and out. There is a whole section of bathroom stalls. I guess they don't have to use the club's bathrooms here.

It's intimidating. The club is huge and there seem to be hundreds of women working. I dance on the stage for two songs and am asked to come down. I am sure that I am not going to get hired since they call me down so quickly. I am granted employment for the coveted eight p.m. til four a.m. shift! I wander around the club from room to room. I feel how tourists who come to New York from a small town for the first time must feel. I am overwhelmed and in awe of the size. There are not only several rooms, there are several stages. This club is not open until four a.m. Its open twenty four hours a day. I snap out of my shock and get to work. There are so many men that I just repeat the same thing over and over. There seems to be no need for long small talk chat sessions here like in New York. "Hi, what's your name? Where you from? Is this your first time in Vegas? It's mine. I should take my dress off and rub my body all over you... that sounds like a good idea, right? Should we do it here or get some more privacy in the back?" I made in one night what it would take me a month to make in a New York borough club. During the day I am a tourist doing things like going to Madame Tussauds Wax Museum. I hit up different all-you-can eat buffets when I want something different from the restaurant near my hotel home.

Push

I get back to New York and am alone all over again. I actually miss the familiar strangers I met in Vegas like the waiter that served me everyday at the restaurant near the hotel. He hooked me up with free dinner one night so I treated him to a free dance one night when he came into the club. The thing I really miss about Vegas is that no one treated me badly when I said that I was a stripper. One cab driver asked if I was visiting. "Yes, from New York. I came to work for a few weeks. I'm a stripper."

"Oh, which club? My wife works at one of the ranches. I gotta go pick her up later. They stay for a week or two at a time to work."

"Oh, wow, I didn't know that. How much do I owe you? Have a nice day."

Now I'm back to this isolated little bubble. It sucks even more now after two weeks of not having to self edit. This morning my head feels like it is going to explode from the force of all of the really awful things I have to say to myself, "What are you so sad about? There are children starving in Africa. There are people living in war zones in some parts of the world. Poor you, you're a stripper, whaaa! You have a safe place to live, you can buy food, both your parents love you. What are you always crying about? GOD, Stop it."

I can't stop the talking. I can't stop the tears. I go to the computer and research a suicide hotline. There will be someone I can talk to on the other line at least. I find a number and call it. I get a recorded message. The number is out of service. Really?!? If I was suicidal that just might be enough to convince me that killing myself just might be a good choice after all. Jeez, not even the suicide hotline cares enough to pick up my call.

I dial another number. I'm put on hold. I'm put on hold to be connected to someone in my area.

"Look, I'm not suicidal… I just…"

"But you said the word suicide."

"I know I said the word suicide but I'm not suicidal."

"How can I help you?"

"I just need someone to talk to… I'm a dancer."

"Oh! A dancer? That's nice."

"Yes, well, not a dancer proper. I'm a stripper and…"

"A stripper?"

"Yes, a stripper. Anyway, I feel SO alone. I feel like I'm about to pop. I don't have anyone talk to about it and I'm so sad and stay in my apartment for days. It's like I'm in this little bubble and my brain is gonna pop"

"Hold on… No, no, no paper not plastic…"

"Are you shopping?!"

"Listen, Sweetie, I'm going to give your information to the psychiatric ER near your house. There's a psychiatrist on call there all the time. What's your name?"

This is the day that I checked myself into a psychiatric ER. This is the day I realized why so many people don't seek out mental health help, especially people of color. This was also the first day on my road towards redemption and self-actualization.

Essence Revealed is a dual degreed former lap dance engineer of the Gentlemen's Club scene, New York to Vegas & sweet places in between. Essence Revealed, the solo play premiered at the 2012 DC Back Theater Festival. Her writing has appeared in $pread,

Corset Magazine, BurlesqueBible.com *and* 21st Century Burlesque. *The burlesque dancer can be seen all over the U.S.A. (solo and with the troupe Brown Girls Burlesque). When not performing, she's empowering women through Sensual Dance & "Bootytwerkaerobics" workshops. www.essencerevealed.wordpress.com*

LD Sorrow

The Time my Dad Found my Business Card

My Dad was in my room looking for something and found my business card. Not the one with my real name, or even my almost-real name, but full fake name, partial nudity. He is now holding this card, the card I use to advertise sexual services, in his hand, and I can tell he wants to talk to me about it. A slow burn in my throat starts to close it. My ears are burning, too. Here he is now, beginning to ask a question, "Do you…"

My body is locked tense in preparation for the worst, my gaze fixed anywhere but my dad.

There's no anger in his voice. Just a cautious suspicion. "I don't mind if you… I don't care who you have sex with. Or what kind of sex you have…"

My brain jumps at a better scenario: maybe he just thinks I'm swinging! Maybe this will get filed with "being a dyke" and "dying my hair weird colors," under "weird things my children did after we didn't raise them Catholic."

Swinging. Maybe that's what he thinks! I nod fiercely to cut him off. "Thanks, Dad. Like…thank you." Full stop, emphasis on the last part of the sentence. Good talk,

Dad, see you out there.

But it's not over. "I don't care about what kind of sex you have. I just…ahh." He tightens his jaw. "I feel a little uncomfortable with you selling it."

Oh my god.

"Yes! Yes! That's okay, Dad. It's okay to be uncomfortable with me, uh, selling sex, Dad."

For an excruciating conversation, I feel pretty good. I feel great! I don't even have to fight being disowned.

"Are you….do you…I hope you don't do the part where they do things to you…like…I would hope you would be…the one doing things to other people."

The tension in my body re-locks in place. I'm not going anywhere.

Maybe my father was angry-- angry enough to exact revenge. Maybe he knew that the only pain beyond a quantitative conversation about sex work—yes, no, how many, how much—was a qualitative one. Open-ended questions. Each requiring their own thoughtful, extended response.

LD Sorrow is a medical professional in NYC and although she has left her life of erotic odd-jobs behind, her Dad still finds unique ways to embarrass her.

Anna Saini

Sin

Sin was tall, lanky, and bald-headed, with sinewy muscles lining his body like survival does the thin-boned people like us. He wore a wide gold hoop earring that hugged his lobe like a confused halo. He wore a puffy leather bomber jacket that was garnished with pink fake fur. I suppose Sin dressed like a pimp. With his bald head and wizened cocoa face I thought he looked more like a Black pirate or a magician. He was baffled that I wasn't scared of him. He liked how it made him feel and, even more than that, it immediately endeared me to him.

He met me in the lobby of his building, the Garrison, on a Friday night as the after hours club on the first floor began to heat up. Strippers began to filter in after their shift ended at the titty bar across the street called the Golden Rail. Smoke from dry ice billowed out and snaked up and around their bodies as each of them entered. I tried to look like I knew what went down in a place like that. I'd been waiting there for coming up to an hour with a round-eyed blonde woman who wore her naiveté like a target.

The building dwellers—some of them who presumably had an apartment at the Garrison, others who were homeless and still others who frequented the after-hours club—circled her hungrily. "Hey baby girl, who you here to see?" "What you doing with Sin when I'm right here for you baby?" Lining her slim stature like a mote were indiscriminate bags of lady clothes composed of spandex, glitter, and feathers. "Oh you gonna get dressed up for Sin to take your picture? I could take your picture for you baby."

We were both recruits of a woman we connected with off of Craigslist, Diana, who sent us to meet with Sin to get pictures done. I went to Diana to help me book my first clients. I was six days late on my rent by then and I had no idea how to set up a trick on my own. I figured if this was how I would get started, giving a hefty cut to a somewhat shady broker, then so be it. She was also getting me this shoot with Sin for free and I would use the pictures to get my own site up eventually, so I could sell myself and keep all my profits.

I stepped to the blonde woman with a somewhat misguided sense that I could act as a buffer between her suburban innocence and the real world of prostitution.

"Leave her alone," I said, with the swagger of a Brown woman cowboy, a cowboy that I doubt has ever existed. There was a twitter of chuckles and a generalized dissipation of interest. There was a parting of seas.

"I'm here to see Sin, too. Any idea where he is? Have you waited here long?"

She diverted her round blue eyes, "Umm... yeah... Diana's on her way, she says she is, you know Diana right?"

There was an air of desperation in the lilt of her voice and then a gasp of relief as Diana blew in, her frizzy Puerto Rican hair in a fog surrounding her with a gust of wind through the front door of the Garrison.

"Sorry I'm late," Diana rattled off a trail of excuses punctuated by words that were her regulars: kids, mutherfucker, dumbshit. She was at the same time fumbling with her phone. "This dumbshit mutherfucker better not be late because I done left my kids at their daddy's to get all the way over to this crack house." Now she was talking to her phone, not us, a fact that was only detectable by the subtle change in her gaze that broke eye contact with us and was directed instead toward the mouthpiece, "Hello? YEAH mutherfucker I'm here. Get your dumbshit ass down here, I been waiting!"

Sin must've already been in the stairwell because he appeared in the lobby just then, sifting through the chaos. "Aight, aight, ok. I'm here. Relax yourself," He was still speaking to Diana through his phone although they were now facing each other and within earshot.

"You're late mutherfucker. Get your dumbshit ass moving. Don't you know I need to pick up my kids."

The blonde woman, whom I'd almost completely forgotten existed, piped up.

"We going upstairs to shoot?" She wanted to get out of the lobby.

Diana looked at me, then the round-eyed blonde, then back at me again. "He'll ride with you."

Sin and I summarily introduced ourselves as we trudged through the unplowed downtown Detroit street to my car parked in the Golden Rail lot. The attendant saw me earlier, slowed down to crawl around the Garrison, looking for a spot on the street. When I asked him how much I owed him to park he flashed me the smile that gives Detroit its nickname, The Deep South in The North. "I can watch your car if you're only gonna be a minute. You shouldn't stay too long if you can help it. And if whoever you here to see doesn't let you in right away you keep it right on movin, ok? Ain't nothing good waiting here for a pretty girl like you."

He was as patronizing as he was kind. It helped that he

was right. Even though we were only a block away from the Fillmore on Woodward, in the heart of the once thriving city, every sidestreet off of the main artery was clogged with desperation. It made me worry for the round-eyed blonde. I was relieved she made it to her car accompanied by Diana.

When we got into my car Sin rattled off directions: "You turn right up here, at the street without a sign, just take your next right don't worry about the name, then get right over to the left because when you get into the traffic circle you want to take the third right..." I responded with a blank stare. "I'll just tell you the way as we go," he said.

Detroit is geographically the largest city in the United States. You can drive for an hour each way on the freeway and still be within the city limits proper. The urban plan is a living testament to the failed optimism of the auto industry. The city is spread out and navigated through a complex network of highways, rubber and steel. Once we were off the convoluted street routes and onto the freeway Sin told me to relax, that we were hanging straight for the next 20 minutes or so to a gallery on Grande Street. Sin interrupted our conversation occasionally with warnings: "Watch the road, the potholes here are like graves."

He asked me what the pictures were for and I told him about the late rent, not knowing how to book clients, my plans for the website. I didn't care enough to lie or conceal even. My instincts told me it was a waste of energy and it was hard enough to avoid the potholes. Sin was right, that's what I needed to worry about most.

"I just want to make my money and get out," I told him. He said yeah he knew what it felt like to be a "porn star" and it wasn't glamorous. "My friends think I don't work for my money. Like fucking ain't work. Like getting your dick hard 10 times a day for every girl they gimme ain't work." He said to me what Diana never would and what few of my fellow workers have admitted to me to this day, "There are so many nights where I cry over what

I lost. I never wanted to fuck for money. Being a porn star or a ho, you make your money but you pay your price too. I wish I could go back." After he died it haunted me the sadness he revealed then, sadness about his lot in life, about ending up in this place. Even if it meant we were here together, it didn't make it any better, just less lonely.

I was still reeling from his admission when I heard him exclaim, "Left, LEFT, LLLLLLEEEEEEFFFFFTTT!!! Girl can't you hear me telling you to hit this left right now goddammit. Shit. Ok now turn quick into this parking lot. I'll jump out and pick up the gate."

I pulled up to the concrete slab of a building that was our destination. It could have been a factory. It probably once was. Now it was a frigid industrial space in the middle of nowhere Detroit that someone, a mutual friend of Diana and Sin's, had converted into an erotic art gallery. Diana and the round-eyed blonde were already there and we both received directions to go to the bathroom and change into our outfits. I let Blondie go first since she was in a rush to get it over with. She changed into a sparkly bathing suit and complained about the cold as she crossed the expansive area from the bathroom to the spot that Sin had set up his gear. Goosebumps trailed her skin like braille reading fear throughout her whole body.

Sin chose as her background a large abstract piece with wrestling pastel shades that complimented the round-eyed woman's straw hair and blue pooling eyes. He gently asked if he could touch her and she demurely nodded yes. He grazed the tips of his index finger underneath the edge of the bikini bottom on either side of her crotch and on the belly so that the fabric lay flat on her body. He untwisted the straps of her top and used his same index fingers to curl into spirals the tendrils of hair around her face. He tamed the fly away strands with his open downward palms.

He pointed toward the velvet couch in front of the abstraction and began clicking to record the natural grace of her movements as she placed herself in a laying position. She could not help but look graceful behind his lens as her self-consciousness dissolved into an air of confidence. Sin himself was moving to the music of his shutter like a waltz. Through the camera display I could see that Sin accomplished what I thought impossible: he made the round-eyed woman look something other than average.

When it was my turn he looked upon the gallery set as he would a used condom. He asked me if I wouldn't mind heading back to his place to shoot. It was after midnight and Diana was long gone dealing with "baby daddy issues" accompanied by a string of curses. Round-eyed Blondie was already half-dressed by the time Sin told her she was done.

"I got some weed there, too," he said as if to seal the deal.

On the drive back to his place Sin told me he hadn't worked doing porn in a while. He would make some money doing shoots like this for Diana and rent was paid for by him working as the building elevator operator. The elevator wasn't particularly safe to ride, which is why it needed someone to operate it and why Sin told most people to take the stairs. He said the Garrison was the Hotel California of Detroit, "You can check out anytime you want, but you can't NEVER leave!"

By the fourth flight up to his apartment Sin told me, heaving and out of breath, that he had a girlfriend up there, sleeping by now, she was pregnant and cranky about him bringing women home, even if it was just for work. The baby wasn't his, he told me, "I just have a bad habit of playing Captain Save-a-Ho," which made him take in any girl he saw who he thought he could help. His pregnant girlfriend was only 19, baby daddy left her, and family didn't want anything to do with her.

Sin didn't have a doorknob. He preferred his door fashioned such that only he could open it by jangling a screwdriver in the mechanism that would normally house the knob. When I entered the apartment I was surprised to find the reason for his elaborate security measures. What Sin hadn't told me was that he was a musician. A drummer, more specifically. The room gravitated around a massive drum kit that was Sin's pride. Orbiting along the walls were framed event fliers advertising shows of the Black Bottom Band, a legendary Detroit act that faded in notoriety by the time I moved to the city.

Sin pulled down a black background from a suspended roll for me to pose in front of. He asked if he could use the baby oil I brought. I was changed into a black thong and heels, a lace corset and garter, a pearl necklace: a classy hooker uniform. He knelt down as if to pray at my altar then squeezed baby oil into his opposite hand. He grazed his palms methodically down the inside of my thighs and ankles, the outside, my backside. He painted my décolletage with oil, moved down my shoulders, and lingered on my hands. He did all of this in the near silence of his smooth, even breath.

With his girlfriend asleep in the loft above and evidence of his celebrity surrounding us, we began to shoot in the palatable aura of sexual tension. It was the proximity and the taboo. I learned the cliché of seducing my photographer through the camera. I took off my clothes one by one, not to reveal what was underneath but to show him that I would do it without him having to ask. The end products reeked of intimacy.

We were done when I couldn't move anymore. I was stiff with aching soreness throughout my abdominals that I had sucked in for Sin and the camera's benefit. I said nothing but he could sense it with his fine-tuned photographer eye in the quiver of my limbs.

"Lay out if you want, we're finished."

I flopped onto my back from my final pose that had me extended out on my side. I let my heels drop off my feet and let the pain radiate throughout me. I let my eyes fall shut to the sight of Sin cradling drumsticks in his palms. I let my mind seek a resting place in the steady beat he gently manipulated out of the kit. I let myself drift off like that, naked and defenseless, on the floor of his makeshift studio.

I awoke pristine and preserved in the same exact position, Sin fluttering above me, stroking my face and cooing, "You ready to go home, pretty lady?"

He picked me up, groggy and disheveled, helped me dress and told me the photos would be ready for me in a few days. The dawn was creeping over the horizon by now, his girlfriend would be awake soon and no doubt unhappy about his choice of overnight guest. He walked me out amongst the Garrison's lobby-dwellers and their heckling our perceived indiscretions. He kissed me on the forehead.

I walked half-way to my car at the Golden Rail before I heard Sin call out to me.

"Hey, Anna, I have to ask you something before you leave! Don't go!"

I turned around expectant of I don't know what, glowing from the flicker of romance. Sin looked straight into my coy face, he looked earnest and he said, "I really hate to ask, but Anna could you lend me some change to buy a pack of cigs?"

"Ugh. No, Sin, I ain't got shit." My expression fell into distaste. I spun on my heel away from him as he yelled into my back, "Sorry! I'm just broke as shit and fiendin' for a smoke."

"It's cool," I said without turning around to look at him, "But I don't got anything for you."

After that, I shot with him a few more times. The shoots got worse as Sin's life spiraled more and more out of favor. Even when Sin was bad, he was good. The photos were useful to fulfill the desire of my growing client list. As I became more established Sin asked me if I would do porn as his leading lady. I told him I wasn't interested. The last time I saw him there was a new woman living there, two live-in girlfriends after the original pregnant one that slept through our first photo shoot. Sin had a gruff attitude toward her that made me for the first time consider that he might actually be a pimp. He tried to get me take pictures with her to help her get work. He took a dying houseplant out from a corner of his bedroom to the rolled down background that was visibly stained with dust. I said I was too tired to shoot, I just wanted to put a blunt in the air if he was down.

He told me his mother was dying of cancer. He told me he had outstanding warrants for unpaid child support. Some drama with the state that had nothing to do with his baby momma. He gave money to her once a month or more depending on what he could afford. He was suspicious of giving it to the system that skimmed off the top of the check that was supposed to go to his daughters. Now he wanted to work a legit job, to support his girls and get out of this life. Meant that he would turn himself in and serve some time. He was done running.

I felt like I was closing in on the end of my run, too. I raised enough money using Sin's pictures to book work so that I could move to New York City. I hadn't lived there before but I'd visited a few times recently and found out that there was a real economy there, with jobs coming up every day. I knew if I tried hard I could get one. I knew if I stayed in Detroit nothing would change. In Detroit, selling sex was one of very few lucrative and stable careers.

All the changes, making my end run, it took all my focus. I stopped returning Sin's texts. They oscillated between persistent and casual, sometimes saying he wanted to be with me, that he would do anything for it, and sometime suggesting we hang out sometime, when I got the chance.

After I got my first job out of sex work—a community organizing gig in Brooklyn, a great fit for me—Sin finally dropped off my radar. I was grateful. He was part of a previous life, a painful and humiliating life where all we could do was temporarily partner with other desperate people.

Months after my move I learned through Facebook that a benefit was planned for Sin. He had stage four lung cancer that was terminal. The benefit was brought together by a group of Detroiters in an effort to honor the city's legendary drummer. It would cover his health expenses as he "transitioned to the ancestor world." I didn't have time to process it or conjure the courage to call him. A week later on the afternoon of the planned benefit there was a post on the event wall saying Sin was gone. He was found "peacefully," it said, and the benefit would "honor him and bring his community together to celebrate his life." Posted was a picture of Sin looking like I never saw him, on the other end of the lens in a tailored vibrant orange zoot suit behind a set of drums backing up the Black Bottom Band on stage at the Fillmore.

Anna Saini has lived many lives as a political scientist, radical activist, and multi-media artist. She completed a B.A. and M.A. in Political Science at the University of Toronto and McMaster University respectively. She works as a community organizer on drug and education policy reform, civil and labor rights, prison abolition, police brutality, and post-colonial feminist liberation. Her work has appeared in Bitch Magazine, Make/Shift Magazine, *various journals and her self-titled anthology* Colored Girls.

Josh Ryley

Fist

The building was large and imposing and sat opposite the armory. There were barred windows all along the first floor and when I peered inside flickering florescent lights and pale green walls met my gaze. I wasn't sure if this was a residence, a halfway house, or worse—some fake address the client had given me over the phone. I had heard of false calls before and while it had not happened to me I always suspected that any day it would be my turn.

Our conversation had been stilted and filled with odd moments of silence along with his heavy breathing and a distinct slapping sound I have come to realize is the sound of masturbation. However he did not "finish" and suddenly hang up, as most time wasting phone callers had: he went on. He was coaxing me into his fantasy, which he finally revealed after I asked for the address and told him I needed to go as I was in a bad area for reception (a trick I use when the conversation seems pointless). He was looking for three hours and he wanted a totally dominant fisting top. Be there promptly at ten, he would provide the necessary accoutrement.

"Can you do this?" he asked in a curt manner.

"Absolutely," I answered in a deep and commanding voice that even I didn't recognize. "And from now on when you address me you will call me SIR. I never want to hear that tone of voice from you again. I expect you to be prepared, clean inside and out. If you aren't you will be punished."

This was new to me. I had never fisted anyone in my life. The idea of having a meat puppet on the end of my hand was more than a bit scary. I knew you could seriously injure a person from shoving your hand where the sun doesn't shine and I did not want to be responsible for an untimely death or complete loss of bowel control. However, three hours meant good money, money I truly needed after a rough week. Aside from the money I could not get this idea out of my head, feeling someone deep inside was so taboo. It required total trust and total control. One wrong turn of my hand and I could rupture a spleen or who knows what else.

I was reaching a new point in my work where each call was bringing on a sexual game of chicken and I was beginning to enjoy the rush. I was being exposed to a number of new fetishes I had not known existed and each one was a lesson in my own desires as well as fulfilling others. How far would I go before I would say I'd gone far enough and I was done? I am not a naturally abusive, aggressively dominant person. I am the type of guy who offers a warm hug and a gentle touch. I listen to my partner, not control them. Although I'd been asked in the past to verbally abuse clients and found that to be a bit titillating, I'd never been asked to perform an act I considered erotically violent; I wanted to play the role.

Now however, when faced with the imposing brick façade and iron bars, I did not feel so daring—I wanted to run. I took a deep breath. When I agree to a job I see it through. I had my pride to contend with and no scared little boy inside was going to get in my way. I texted my safety, told him where I was and that if he didn't hear from me by one a.m. to call. If I didn't respond by two a.m., I said, call the cops.

As I pushed open the glass door of the building, I was met with the smell of disinfectant and urine. A dim light flickered from brown to yellow over my head. The stout woman behind the glass wore a brown security guard uniform and had a taser gun attached to her belt. This was a far cry from the upscale apartment buildings I had been visiting where I was greeted by courtly gentlemen in fine suites who smiled while opening the door.

"Name, ID and who you seein,'" she said without looking up from her tiny portable television.

I was not aware I had to give my ID as I was using my professional name and began to panic. My mouth went dry.

"I... I have an ID but my buddy knows me by my middle name and... I just..."

"Honey, I don't care, just sign this and let me see your ID, I don't call up, if he's expecting you, he's expecting you. I ain't no doorman!" Hooting with laughter as she lifted her large ass from the chair, she snatched my ID from my hand and scribbled something in a book, then shuffled back to the chair shaking her head.

If she wasn't a doorman who the hell was she and what the fuck was this place? I should have run but I was even more intrigued by what lay behind the glass door and a tingle of uncertain excitement was causing the hairs on the back of my neck to stand up.

My legs moved on autopilot as she buzzed me through the second glass door. The lobby had an even stronger smell of disinfectant, more along the lines of a cheap urinal cake. There were a few ratty chairs huddled around an old table and in the corner stood a small sad excuse for a Christmas tree, its wire limbs each going in unnatural directions. Garish bright lights blinked showcasing the few glittering ornaments left still clinging to the synthetic pine needles. There were old paper wreaths and chubby Santa faces taped up to the wall with yellowing scotch tape. I swore I heard a faint scream in the distance and my legs locked. I could still leave, he would never know, but a voice inside me said, "Do it! See what's on the other side! You'll never know unless you try!" It's true, I would never know and I hated not knowing, I hated failure. My motto has always been "if anyone can do it, I can."

I was jilted back to reality by a pounding on the glass behind me.

"Stairs are to your left sweetie, OKAY? Elevator is broken."

I slowly moved towards the stairs, checking my breath, fixing my hair, moving all my valuables into zippered hidden pockets in my bag. As I reached the top of the first landing, I noticed that the colors of the walls did not change, the building did not get nicer and there was a distinct medical/nursing home vibe to it. Pale hospital green walls surrounded me. There were dirty trays of half-eaten food outside doors, American flags hanging on the walls, tattered paper candy canes on doors, doors left wide open with televisions blasting, but not a person in sight. I held my head up and got ready to assume my dominant persona: Josh the fisting power top. Josh wouldn't not let this shit get to him. Josh would command the space, he would pound his Timberland boots down the hall and let his presence be known. Most importantly I WAS Josh and I was not going to let the color of a wall and a strange building that smelled like piss get to me.

I reached his door and knocked. A series of dogs barked and a cat meowed. It sounded like a zoo. The door slowly creaked opened.

"I'm not fully ready Sir, you will have to wait for me to set up. Come in," a meek voice called from the other side. This was a common tactic for clients who thought of themselves as unattractive. They would hide behind the door until you were inside, then close it behind you as if saying, "can't run now." The craziest thing about this, I always thought, was why would I run? They were paying me to be there and whether or not they were attractive didn't matter to me. I was there to do a job.

I tried to take control and push the door open but quickly realized this was not a client ploy, the door was blocked by something other then a person. As I shimmed through the crack I was greeted by junk—floor to the ceiling boxes. I started to panic. Tight junk-filled spaces and I do not get along. It is a fear of mine to be smothered in rubble from trash, a deep unfounded fear that to this day I don't fully understand but it's the reason that, twice a year, I go through my apartment and throw out everything I haven't touched in six months.

I swallowed hard and told myself, "If anyone can do this I can."

His tall, thin frame filled the tiny passageway as he led me through the rubble. We passed a filthy bathroom on my right with cat litter covering the floor, empty toilet paper rolls strewn about and several dirty towels were dangling off of hooks. He had reached the end of the tunnel where he moved out of the way to let me into his space. With the dogs yapping at my feet and the cat twining through my legs I took the few steps into the apartment.

It was a small studio with a corner kitchen. Towers of debris teetered everywhere. It not only sounded like a zoo, it smelled like one, too. There were boxes filled with books, books filled with papers, cat litter boxes filled with dog food, dog food bags filled with fabric brimming from their tops. Stacks of speakers rose next to nests of wires, and the most striking thing to me was the number of old computers lying around with wee wee pads (the dog equivalent of a cat box) on top of them. Not just plain old wee wee pads mind you but dirty wee wee pads. My eyes adjusted to the light and I saw the mangy dogs at my feet, they were mutts and not very well groomed. The cat had a patch of fur missing from its back. I felt sorry for these little guys and my heart began to melt as I knelt down to pet one of them and was greeted by a snarl. I jumped back in shock and then remembered, I am "power fisting, dominant, aggressive Josh." I gave the dog a dirty look, stood up and stepped over him to show him who was boss and to get a better look at my host who had finally turned around.

He was in his late forties and looked like he had smoked most of his life. His skin was grey and pasty. His dirty blonde greasy hair kept falling over his dull and glassy pale blue eyes. I could see something deep inside them, a spark that had been buried over time. I lowered my eyes and noticed he was dressed in a loose fitting t-shirt and a jockstrap. His pancake ass flapped in the breeze with each nervous step he took. He sat me down in a big, overstuffed dirty leather office chair.

"Just let me get this all set up, Sir, and put my friends in the bathroom."

His giant flat screen TV played *The Simpsons* and I felt solace in the fact that my favorite television show was on keeping me company like a friend. I could take a quick breath and get my bearings about me before I had to continue.

He pushed a number of boxes off something and revealed a futon that he then unfolded. It filled most the room. Surprisingly, it was not dirty and actually the cleanest thing in his place. He shooed the dogs and cat into the bathroom and closed the door. He turned, faced me and smiled.

"Thank you for coming, Sir…"

"You're welcome. I have a question though: what is this place?"

"An apartment building."

"Really? I've never seen a building like this… is it a home for war veterans or—"

"ITS AN APARTMENT BUILDING!"

He put his hands on the counter facing away from me and took a series of deep breaths. His droopy ass was shaking. I could have assumed the dominant role and yelled back but I was stunned at his change in demeanor. This guy wasn't right and I did not know what he was capable of. His frail frame could hide some freakish notion of strength and he was in the kitchen with easy access to knives and sharp objects.

After a few beats he continued, "It's an apartment building that used to be medical offices…" with that, he went back to his activity in the kitchen corner. It appeared he was mixing something in a bowl with water, like a happy homemaker preparing a cake.

"I have the gloves over there, Sir. I would like to start out with toys and work my way up to your fist. I'm making the J-lube and it'll be ready in a second so feel free to get undressed."

"What's J-lube?"

"It's lube that's used in gynecological examinations for farm animals." He placed the bowl in the microwave. "I like to warm it up a bit."

With that he turned and smiled as if he'd just said, "My secret ingredient is a dash of nutmeg—shhhhh don't tell anyone!"

Farm lube?! What happened to simple "boy butter"— the lubricant I had often seen in sex store windows that made me think of happy twinks milking cows to make an all natural lube for their tender hairless asses. Why animal lube used for cow vaginas? My stomach was sinking and I checked the clock. Only 15 minutes had passed. This would be a long three hours.

I repeated my mantra, "If anyone can do this I can."

"I'll need you to put on the gloves, then add the lube to your hand. Once you lube my ass you need to pull out and put this on it and rub it on the inside of my rectum"

He handed me a small brown bottle with a powder in

55

it.

"What is this?" I was losing control of the situation. I was not being a dominant top.

"Coke. I want you to put it in my ass—if you want some you are welcome."

"I'm sober," I lied, although it was true I didn't do drugs with clients. Clients are unpredictable enough on drugs that why would I choose to further complicate my situation by being fucked up as well? It was also true that I hated coke.

"Your loss, but you don't mind doing it, do you?"

"No! I asked you to call me SIR and if you mess up again I WILL LEAVE!" Dominant Josh was back.

"Oh no! You can't leave, please don't!" He was almost crying right when the microwave dinged.

"Sounds like we're ready," he smiled. His emotions turned like a light switch.

Returning to the living room, he changed the station to some porn-- not the nice, pretty studio porn or even amateur, it was harsh dungeon, extreme kink porn. As the movie came on the screen, a guy was shoving a bat into his ass while a metal rod protruded from his urethra in a factory setting.

He pulled out the box of gloves and toys from under the futon then placed several fresh wee wee pads and placed them on the bed.

"I don't like to be messy!"

This was the last thing I expected from a man whose apartment looked like it exploded. I didn't say anything. Instead, I sat in silence as he laid out the toys from smallest butt plug to traffic cone sized black silicone battering ram. The styrofoam bowl, which he'd placed a spoon in, was placed at the end of the line-up.

"Please start small, Sir, then work up. I'd like to suck your cock while we begin."

I slowly undressed as he lay there with his ass up in the air. I can usually find something to turn me on but I was intimidated by all the instructions and nothing was working. I hoped that my flaccid cock would get hard once some friction hit it but he wasn't getting my usual, "Surprise I'm ready!" moment. It further deflated my ego and I took a breathe closed my eyes and thought, "Tough as nails, tougher then Joan Crawford, tougher then Hillary Clinton, tougher then a Drag Queen…" I had to stop, as gay man yes, I knew these were ball busting tough figures but this was not that kind of night. I looked at his skin flap ass, the toys, and closed my eyes again and thought "Tougher then a drill sergeant, then a navy seal, Rambo, Arnold Schwarzenegger, The Hulk…The Hulk with his massive green angry muscles and ripped pants getting angry at Arnold, they are fighting and now, they are making out with Rambo in a three way as the wrestle to the ground…" There it was, I was getting hard.

I picked the spoon out of the Styrofoam bowl and the thick, sickening lube made a slurping sound like the blob. I covered the smallest toy and began to work his hole.

"Wait, Sir, wait! The coke, please the coke!!" He was whining and I hadn't even touched him. "Also, just start with a finger."

I snapped on a glove and watched the medical powder fly. I placed some of the warm lube on my hand and sprinkled some of the coke from the brown bottle he had given me on top. It was sticky… this was not good coke. I hated coke because I knew coke. I had done my share in my early twenties. I knew the good stuff was very powdery and crystal like. The stuff cut with baby laxatives and other shit clumped and stuck together. I was worried about what it would do but not enough to stop as I followed his request.

The position was awkward, his ass up, head down, trying to suck my dick as I stood from the side trying to reach his ass at the end of his long torso but finally he lost interest in my dick and I went towards the back. In went the finger.

"Oh, I am so tight, Sir, it hurts!" He buried his head in the pillow. He was far from tight; his ass was already gaping in the air. Most gaping clients declare their tight virgin asses couldn't handle things when really you could drive a truck in and they wouldn't notice.

"Yes you're one TIGHT, DIRTY, BAD man--"

"Boy!" he shouted

"Boy?! Boy what?" I shouted back, topping his cry in my butchest, deepest voice yet.

"Boy... SIR," his asshole winked at me, I could tell he liked being yelled at.

"Yes you are one tight boy, you have been bad and need to pay."

I added more coke and continued with my fingers, one, two, then three rubbing the inside of his rectum. I then grabbed one of his over sized dildos and began to work the tip in.

"You NASTY boy, you are FUCKED UP and here comes something to make you pay." I shoved the large dildo in, not gently, harshly and hard and to my surprised, it was swallowed up like a hot dog at a hot dog eating competition.

"Oooo my tight ass... Ooo, Sir, you are being too good to me. Thank you, Sir!"

I figured the more toys I played with the less time I had to spend fucking him, so I went back and forth and back and forth—the large one, the long one, the fat one the short one until finally he said, "Your hand, Sir, I think I need an internal spanking!"

I tried not to laugh and braced myself as I lubed up my hand over my glove, placed a layer of coke on it and noticed my fingers were going numb—the shit was leaking through my glove! It was too late now. At an hour and fifteen in, I could do it. I was doing it. I was facing this fucking challenge head on and saying, "Show me what you got life, I can handle it!"

I started with my fingers... one, two, three, four...

then my whole hand, massaging the coke in. I then balled up my fingers and pushed until the eager toothless mouth swallowed my fist. I almost passed out at the sensation of warm innards sliding by my clenched hand. My erection was gone but the hairs on my body tingled. I could feel his whole body pulsing on my fist.

"Now punch it, Sir!"

I pulled out my first and went full force, punching his asshole with all my might. It went right in but he jolted up and to attention.

"Oh my oh my oh my oh my!"

I took my hand out and he stood up, a trail of J-lube hanging off his ass and a wee wee pad stuck to that followed behind him as he circled around in the kitchen corner.

"That was great that was great that was great!"

He was all sped up as he turned away from me and bent into a drawer and took a deep sniff of something and then came back.

"More, Sir, I have been really bad, more coke, too, please!"

Again, I lubed up my hand, added the coke and punched into his ass then opened my hand inside and lined his walls. He moaned and winced. I pushed deeper past my wrist.

I couldn't stop. The voice inside said, "Why are you doing this? This is not you!" but the strong-willed hardass part of me punched that other part down. I was doing it because I could. I was in control. I pushed on, deeper and deeper, feeling his organs shift and move until a squeal came from the man.

"That's too far too far too far! I don't like deep fisting, up to your wrist only—you were doing a great job!"

I retracted my soaked arm and he got up and went back to the corner, wee wee pad and lube tail in tow. He sniffed hard and lay back down.

Once he was settled, I decided to lay into him. "Shut

the fuck up I heard you and I know I'm doing a great job. You think I NEED your APPROVAL! Put your head down and shut the fuck up, boy."

With that, I spanked him, hard. My hand left a big red mark on his boney ass. I felt bad for leaving a mark.

"Yes, Sir!"

In out and around, in out and around, I was getting the hang of it, getting a good rhythm—right when he stopped me and said, 'I want your cock."

My dick, at this point, was not interested in any of these goings-on, but I knew I had to do something, and so I said, "You fist yourself, and show me what a big boy you are and I will fuck you."

He turned his face up towards mine, grinning ear to ear. He flipped himself over on his back, reached around and in went his hand. I stood there looking at him while I fluffed myself up. I noticed the porn behind him had changed scenes and now a guy was being double fucked, I got hard again.

I held his legs up with my shoulders and rolled on my condom. It was like fucking a garbage bag. There was no friction, just a warm void. Then my dick went numb, which was a blessing, as it kept it hard. I pounded him, feeling my pelvis smack against his ass bones. Then I switched rhythms and movements going in a circular motion. I continued to fuck him in this piston style when I noticed his eyes rolling in the back of his head. At first I thought, "Yeah he likes this... I am the man." Then I noticed his eyes were not coming back. It was not the roll of good feelings but of something going wrong.

His face had gone from grey to white. His lips were turning blue.

I pulled out and wiped his ass with one of the wee pads he had set out. He wasn't moving and his legs fell limp as did my dick and I slid off the condom. I went to his face and lightly slapped him.

"Hey man, hello, hey, hey hey, you okay? Wake up

please, wake up."

He wasn't waking up. I started shaking. This poor man was dead, he was dead and I was a hooker sitting in his hoarder apartment and the woman downstairs knew my real name. I couldn't leave him there for his dogs to eat—that would just be awful, I would have to call 911 or get that woman or whatever wardens are in this psychiatric halfway house to help me and just say I am a friend. I had to think fast and remembered who I was but I was at a loss until I remembered—this was not me. I was power fisting Josh. This Josh does not lose control.

"COME ON MAN, WAKE UP!" I wound my hand back and smacked him with all my might, harder then I had ever hit anyone in my life. His eyes fluttered and he gave me a confused look.

"Wait, what happened..." He tried to stand up. "Oh my god I am spinning," he whispered as he collapsed and started to close his eyes again.

"No no no, stay with me buddy, sit up, come on, that's a good boy, sit up."

The real me came back to life, the butch act was vanquished like an evil spirit and the high was over. I had gone too far and I was now forced to face the reality of what I was in. I sat him up on the bed and held him in that position. I was relying on my faded knowledge from the CPR class I took to get out of gym my freshman and sophomore years of high school, and health class lectures on overdoses. I thought of friends who rolled too hard or drank too much—what the fuck did I do with them?

"What were you sniffing over there? You have to tell me! What was that other thing you took?"

"It was K, I was taking K, too... the coke didn't seem to work so I took some K." He looked up at me, sheepish and ashamed.

"Okay, that's okay." I stroked his head and pushed his matted greasy hair away from his sweaty brow.

"What else did you take? Anything else?"

"No just that, it usually is great... just that... it usually..." He was trailing off again. Flecks of foam had formed in the corners of his mouth.

"Hey buddy, listen to me, don't close your eyes, okay? We need to get you something to drink. Do you have any orange juice?"

I had become parental. Coke and K... I don't think it will kill you but then again this was bad coke and I wasn't sure what else was in it. I knew that with ecstasy there was something about drinking orange juice, or was that diabetics? It didn't matter, I figured it would do some good to get some sugar in him or at least a liquid.

"There's orange juice in the fridge. I can get it." He tried to stand up and but couldn't.

"No, you can't. Tell me where your glasses are and I'll pour you some, stay upright and stop taking anything okay, please, PLEASE don't take anything."

I propped him back up against the frame of the futon as I went to the kitchen to get him a drink.

As he we weakly put the glass to his lips and began to drink, I could tell he was coming to. His face was coming back to its grayish tint from the pale white it had been and the color was returning to his lips. We sat in silence while I held his hand.

"I'm sorry," he said in a sad voice staring off into the distance.

"Don't be sorry." I felt sorry for him.

A minute or so later, still holding his hand, I told him I thought our session was over. I assumed that since he passed out and almost overdosed he would agree and send me on my way.

"I guess you're right," he said reluctantly, "but I'm not paying you for three hours."

I let go of his hand. My face turned red. This dumb fuck that could have died was now trying to negotiate my fee with me? He had a lot of nerve!

A part of me understood. Clearly he was not a man

with a lot of money to throw around. He had probably saved up for this night for a while. In any case, I didn't want to be the asshole that freaks out and demands money. The job was over. I just wanted to leave.

Out the door and down the hall, down the stairs and past the security guard and into the cool fresh winter air, a wave of what had just happened came over me. I got to the end of the block, stopped, and I cried.

After a few moments I wiped away my tears and pulled my phone out from the secret pocket. I texted my safety that I was done. I did not share the details when asked; I just repeated, "I'm done."

Josh Ryley is an escort living in New York City. He has been nominated for several "Hookies" (the escort awards sponsored by rentboy.com) including Mr. New York and Best Newcomer. He has read at, hosted, and curated nights for The Red Umbrella Diaries and is currently the editor for the RedUP podcast He would like to thank Audacia Ray and Melissa Petro for giving him the opportunity to express himself and refine his voice.

Lovely Brown

Mr. John and Me

"Take off your panties," John commands me with a wildness in his eyes that I have grown to love.

These were the words I've been waiting to hear all week. I dutifully did as I was told, after all, I was being paid for a service. As I follow his orders and bent myself over his knee I can see the excitement growing inside of him. He sat still for a moment just looking down at me.

"Have you lost weight?" he asks me while caressing my bare backside.

"Um, I don't know. Have I?"

"Yeah, it looks like you have."

John has a thing for chubby brown girls and loves my body but I'm happy that all those hours in the gym are finally paying off. I secretly smile inside. I am really going to get it now.

He caresses my backside gently as I close my eyes and wait for what is to come next. Quick as a flash he raises his hand and smacks the underside of my bottom. With that one fell swoop motion begins our weekly dual spanking and sex session.

John was the first person I traded sex with for money. We met on Craigslist, the same place I met most of my customers at first. I first got the idea of sex for money from a few college classmates who were also sex workers. I was taken aback at first when they performed writing inspired by their experiences in our solo performance class, but they seemed pretty well adjusted. How bad could it be?

At the time I was drowning in school debt and my rent was almost two months late. Panicked, a few days before the 1st of the month, I decided to take the plunge. It was risky but what did I have to lose? Of course I worried about my safety but my biggest fear was actually: what if no one responds? I posted a suggestively worded ad with a few faceless photos and waited. Curvy ebony student in need of a helping hand from a respectful and generous older gentleman. Within minutes I had nearly 20 responses from men ranging in age from 24 to 45 who were looking for an hour of my time in exchange for "roses," a colloquialism for money in the escort industry.

John was one of the first responses I got. I wish I could say his stood out to me in some magical way but it didn't. He seemed the most sane and respectful of the responses so I choose him to be my first. After a brief phone conversation during which we cryptically negotiated logistics like money and where we would meet, plans were made for him to pick me up near the UC Berkeley campus, where he would then take me to one of his homes in San Rafael.

I climb into the car and notice he appears to be just as nervous as I am. Scanning me up and down with his eyes, he seems pleased and some of my fears are put to rest. John is a thin white man with brown undertones to his skin, courtesy of his father's Guatemalan heritage. He is dressed plainly. A blue t-shirt with nondescript blue jeans and tennis shoes. His shoulder-length brown hair is pulled into a ponytail. He's not bad looking. Probably not someone I would go for in my everyday life, but not bad.

Meeting a perfect stranger for the first time, for the express purpose of having sex has to be one of the most awkward experiences ever. For the next 35 minutes John and I verbally tap dance from subject to subject, discussing anything besides the obvious reason I am with him. He tells me about his time spent building houses in Guatemala and I tell him about what life is like as a recent Midwest transplant.

John: I don't do this when I'm in a relationship, you know.

Me: Oh really? Well why do you do it then?

John: It's just easier you know. Than going out, trying to meet someone and all of that at a bar or something. It gets tiring and honestly, at 38, I'm too old for that shit.

Finally after quite a bit of driving we get to his place. His house is located in a quiet, unassuming suburban neighborhood. Once inside I make a beeline for the bathroom to freshen up and give myself a mini pep talk. Everything is going to be fine, I keep reminding myself. People meet in clubs and bars and go home with each other all the time. How is this any different? The fact that I'm getting paid? All the better then. No big deal, I tell myself. In my head I'm talking big, but in my heart I still didn't know. I'm scared. Here I am miles and miles away from home, alone with a strange white man, getting ready to engage in prostitution. There's no turning back and all I can do is hope for the best and make sure I know of a few different exit strategies in case shit gets real.

After a few minutes I am finally ready. I exit the bathroom and make my way to the living room where he is waiting. I straddle his lap, we began to kiss, and not before long, my red fishnet dress is on the floor next to my clear platform stripper heels. Laying on my back with him looking into my eyes, I really like it when he touches me and kisses my body all over. I can't remember the last time someone has used such a tender touch with me in real life. As he kisses his way down towards my stomach, I can tell he really knows his way around a woman's body. I feel free and wanted. I am 21 and the last time I had sex I was a teenager, 17 years old to be exact. Teenage boys are hardly known for their lovemaking skills.

Meeting up with John became a semi-regular thing. Sometimes he would call me out of the blue wanting me to come over. Other times we would have exact days and times in place weeks in advance. Even when he called me last minute I was usually more than willing to bail on other guys for a chance at being with him. Sure, some of the other guys might have offered more money than John was able to, but at least with him I knew what I was getting.

"Did you miss me?" he asks as I crawl towards him on all fours.

"Yes," I reply, smiling and nodding coyly before finally reaching his lap and assuming my usual position.

I told John I was a full time student who was doing this only in the pursuit of education. That explanation was mostly true. Initially the money was the biggest draw but eventually, I grew to like being someone else's fantasy. Growing up I was the awkward, chubby, new girl who liked to read books and listen to white people music. These men were having sex with me and paying me for it. As an escort for hire I was finally the object of desire. It's a fun thing to think about and revel in as an unsure-of-herself 21 year old. But no matter how much of a thrill I got from the attention those men gave me, it wasn't real. They only wanted me for one thing and after their hour was up, they too were up and out the door. And if they couldn't get what they wanted from me, well, there was always another woman ready and willing. At times it felt good knowing these men were attracted to me but at other times not so much. Outside of escorting my sex and dating life were pretty non-existent. Most of the time I felt invisible to guys and most others around me. No one ever asked me out on dates and when they did the experience was less than stellar.

I remember going on a few dates during that time with Kyle, an older brother of a friend of mine. We were having dinner at some fancy restaurant in the Jack London square district of Oakland, discussing whatever, when the topic of relationships came up. It had been forever since I had been out on a real date and I was feeling butterflies in my stomach. "We get along great, Lovely. You would be perfect for me, except," he paused and then continued, "well, looks do matter. I mean, you're cute and all, but it's not like 'wham, bam, thank you ma'am.'"

I was mortified. It wasn't just in my head. I really was ugly. Afterwards, we caught a movie, *Mission Impossible III*, and I went home feeling even lower than I thought was possible.

Later that Sunday, I was vegging out around my apartment, one half of me waiting on a gentleman caller, one half of me not wanting to be bothered. I look down at my phone as John's number blinked green.

"Hello," I answer, trying to muster my best sick, damsel in distress voice.

"Hey, it's John. Are you available today?"

I hesitate for a second, I could always use the money but ultimately I just don't feel up to it.

"Nah," I respond. "I'm feeling a little under the weather today. Sorry."

Almost without skipping a beat he said, "Oh, okay," and hung up the phone.

I sat there for a moment, stunned. I don't know exactly what it was I was expecting. It wasn't like John was my boyfriend or anything. He had no obligation to care about the fact that I wasn't feeling well that day. Still, I felt saddened that he hadn't even bothered to ask what was wrong. It was in that moment I realized how truly alone I felt when real life happened. There was always someone there when I was horny, but what about when I wanted my back rubbed, or when I got into an argument with my mother? There was no one calling during those times. Just myself, alone on a mattress on the floor of my one bedroom apartment.

I had been escorting for almost nine months and the novelty of trading sex for money was beginning to wear off. I wanted real intimacy, I wanted a man to want to be with me for free, and not just for sex. I couldn't have that if I was still pimping out my body after class. In the fall of 2008 I applied and was accepted to Columbia University in New York City. It was decided, I was moving to the east coast. I never wanted to move to New York but this whole California thing wasn't working out anymore. I moved there to be a college student, not a whore. I needed a fresh start and a full scholarship was just the ticket I was looking for. In the end, I stopped escorting just as easily as I had started. At first I marketed myself as a non-pro, a normal girl who was just looking for extra tuition money. But as time went on, it became harder and harder for me to pretend I was still new to the game. I grew impatient with the constant price haggling, tired of constantly being on call for total strangers, and I was over trying to pretend I was attracted to balding middle-aged men, who had stomachs that entered the room before they did.

By the time that I moved out of my apartment in Berkeley I had mostly stopped taking new clients. I stayed in my apartment one last night before turning in the keys.

John called that afternoon wanting to see me before I left town. I said yes. He came over and like a ritual, I painted my face, put on my long black wig, and changed into a red fishnet dress. Once inside my bedroom, like a ritual, he asked me to take off my wig, get on all fours, and crawl to him. We had sex one last time and then that was it.

Lovely Brown is a writer living in New York. She has written for: Bust Magazine, Bitch Magazine, Time Out Amsterdam Magazine *and* Alt Variety Magazine *to name a few.*

Marcia Chase

A First Day at an All Boys' Boarding School

That morning I woke to the song by Jimmy Cliff, "I can see clearly now." I jumped out of bed and my eyes did the once over. When will I see you again, old room?

My mom came in, screaming, "The car is waiting for you out front! Call me at once when you arrive at school!" With that she turned, and without notice, had disappeared.

The limousine was white, not huge but elegant. I felt knots in my stomach. I said, "Damn you mom and dad. I'll get you when you're old. I'll stick you both in different homes. Like you did to your children for the sake of your sacrifice."

The driver was a stout man with a beautiful smile, perfect teeth when he smiled. It was as if he wore jewelry on his teeth. They sparkled and gleamed at my eyes. He stood five-foot-four, immaculately dressed, in a British made gray suit. Polished shoes, wing tips. He was so neat. "Must be gay," I said to myself.

He was helpful and careful. After glancing me over, he gave me what felt like a word of advice. He said candidly,

"You are gonna have lots of fun."

I arrived in Barbados and the beauty of the island struck a chord in my soul. I said, "If I was to die I would want to be here." The greenery stretched for miles. There were clusters of trees, thickets, small, medium, and grand foliage. Palm trees, coconuts, all sorts of vegetation of colors danced to the rhythm of the Caribbean. The menagerie of splendor gave a wonderment to my child-like inner spirit of newness.

As the car took the long driveway leading towards Harrison Boys' School, the scenic views were intoxicating. There, hardly visible to decipher, a plaque was nailed to a tree. Must have been a dedication of sort. Never cared to educate myself about this. Coming into focus was the boys' of Harrison. There were lots of them scattered as far as the eye could see. There were tall ones, short ones, afros, curly hair, blondes, a stout one. Thick ones and let's not forget my favorite, the attractively built ones. Their legs and thighs made my heart skip a beat. In my damned mind, as my father would say, I wondered what they looked like underneath their uniforms.

They wore uniforms. Again, I thought, "Damn you, Mom!" They stood before me in khaki shorts, white short sleeves, white long tube socks. Navy blue jacket. A checkerboard tie. One the left pocket was an insignia of a school charter. Again, why would my parents do this to me? When was I gonna be able to wear my pleated skirt and my Mary Janes? Oh hell no, I am not going to like it here. In a flash my mind returned to what the driver had said, " You are gonna have a lot of fun here."

To my surprise, it was at Harrison that I met my first love. That very day, he came over and extended his hand. He spoke to me in a true Bajan accent with all authenticity. "My name is Calvin Thompson," he said, "It's a pleasure to meet you." I was enamored with the sound of his voice. I was in love. He was as black as midnight. Tall with an athletic build. His face was round and very masculine. He was three years my senior. Muscular, I could see his defined chest and stomach muscles. His legs were huge, strong, and lengthy. He was maybe a runner but no, he played cricket. His smile was huge. Perfect. His mouth: beautiful, large teeth.

He would become the most helpful boy at school, from that very day helping me to get comfortable with the surroundings. This jet black adonis become my conquest for the next three years. I was to make this man-boy into my slave if you may. Queens usually only have a short reign. We rule for a few short years and slowly our power is relinquished to other fairies.

I was smitten, wondering if my queenly powers would come to good use—like getting homework done, or like getting into his pants. Putting my hands in his pants, pulling his shorts off. Or maybe sneaking into the bushes and having another discovery session. Can you imagine what boys do at boarding school?

Marcia Chase is a transgender writer living in the Bronx.

Dana Wright

The First Time I Stripped

The first time I stripped I was eighteen and living in Boston. I had followed my high school friend there after running away from home the year before. I didn't have the worst upbringing imaginable but in adolescence everything seems more urgent than it really is. Anyway, my friend from high school was dating a girl named Anita. Anita was an Indian girl from a traditional family and her way to rebel was by dating only black men. I met her partner in crime Kinlayah the summer after they both graduated from Wellesley. While Anita was straying away from further rebellion, Kinlayah was looking for more. Feather boas, glitter, and the thirty-year-old boyfriend she was mostly supporting wasn't enough. They set up in Cambridge near the mall and rented out a room to me in their new apartment for the summer. I was working as a waitress at IHOP on the graveyard shift, trying my best to avoid all responsibility of a busier and probably more profitable time slot.

Kinlayah first posed the idea when I was still seventeen

but it didn't make sense to me. When I thought of strippers I thought of chicks in Motley Crue videos: blonde, fluffy hair, and big boobs. I had neither quality. The idea was separate from the little self-image I had at that age so the idea was absurd to me. I had a boyfriend at the time. A bored twenty-five-year-old super senior who was enjoying an extended adolescence at MIT on his father's dime, sometimes taking sparse freelance computer consulting jobs to feed the drug experimentation. I wouldn't say addiction, as it was just more about the level of different things he could be on. Speed, coke, special k, Robitussin, there was never a real preference. Garbage head, I think it's called. His friends were fellow MIT super seniors with drug problems, people of an outer section of people—mostly ravers who used his apartment to shoot K.

I did most of the other stuff in tandem with the boyfriend. One night I came over to his house after work and instead of the usual cast of ravers there was a different crowd, a different vibe. There were people there I would normally never see in this environment or hang out with. They were older. They were sitting next to each other but some had their eyes closed and they seemed in their own worlds. Some were slowly swaying as if to their own personal song. The peace that flowed from them was enviable, especially to someone who had sprung from a psychiatric ward just the year before. Whatever they were on, it looked way better than Prozac.

When I tried it, I experienced a calm and content never available to me in my always-unstable existence. After the summer, my dealer sensed our growing dependence and doubled his price for a bundle. It became like a baby to support our habit and suddenly stripping was not so far off a concept. About two months after my 18th birthday my friend and I split a cab out to Malden, a town about a half hour out of Boston.

I Had an Ex-Boyfriend

I had an ex-boyfriend who couldn't get into my job and hated every minute of it. Not at first, but with most men once they start to care about me, I become an entity they want to protect and my job as a stripper lands me on the wrong side of madonna-whore. Not what they want out of a girlfriend. But by then I have fallen in love and then my lover becomes my adversary.

I met Dave at one of the many bars I frequented in Williamsburg after work in an effort to drink myself to sleep. It's pretty hard to wind down after a night working in a strip club. One night my usual watering hole was closed already and I had to go to the bar parallel to it which was never my first choice because the bar I liked always had female bartenders and a more comfortable environment. The wooden Irish style pub I ended up having to go to had bristly guys and other assorted hipsters. That meant a girl covered in a full face of makeup after a night working as a stripper could expect nothing but harm.

But alas, I needed to sleep. When I got there, the bartender was a six-foot-four, over-200-pound white guy with thinning hair and blue eyes. His meathead appearance meshed with the general vibe of the bar and people would later say that his look should have been a tip off to the abuse I would experience. He was easy going and had been a bartender since he dropped out of college, which I later found out was fifteen years before. As we started to talk, I told him about my job, as I'm usually not as secretive with nightlife people. He was a legal drug dealer after all. He told me that his ex-girlfriend's sister was a stripper and it seemed as if he was close enough to my lifestyle to understand.

I started to visit him every Monday and would drink for free. He seemed to appreciate my company and he was good at warding the goons off which made me feel safe. I had very few men who felt protective towards me and I loved the feeling. The world felt less harsh. But as time went on he began building his own ideas on the business I'm in. One day, he showed me an article written by Ice-T about his years as a pimp. This alienated me further, as I was a stripper not a prostitute. It also portrayed prostitutes as victims, something with which I don't necessarily agree. Another common experience with men I would date, Dave would stay mum about my job until just before I had to go to work.

One day, I finally stood up for myself and pointed out that, just like him, I had a job and that he should respect it, just as I respected his.

"Job? You don't have a job," he spat at me, "you have a slut fantasy!"

I didn't know what to say back. Maybe he was right. My job and the loneliness it can cause had managed to erode my self-esteem and I started to believe him. I allowed him to become my voice of reason.

Dana Wright has worked as an exotic dancer for the past fourteen years. As an adolescent, she worked for a news service called Children's Express, a UNICEF program that encouraged young people to speak up on issues that affect them. Through this program, Wright conducted interviews with national leaders including Al Sharpton and David Dinkins, and visited Bosnia and Croatia to interview children on the effects of war.

Veronica Vera

Cherry Pop

As soon as someone learns that I've been a porn star, the first question is always, "How did you get into that business?" Jamie Gillis, star of over 1500 hardcore movies gave the best answer to this frequently asked question when he said, "I was just one of a group of guys playing poker, then l one day I looked at my hand and the naked guy fucking the girl on the back of the deck was me." I bet Jamie remembered a lot more about how it all began. I know I do.

After college, I left the glorious Garden State of New Jersey and travelled to New York to fulfill my dream to be a writer. It was a geographical distance of just 15 miles but it felt more like 1500 if measured in degrees of sophistication. I applied at numerous publishing houses but after failing numerous typing tests, I took a job in Wall Street where I didn't need to type. For a while, this little hick was caught up in the fact-paced, glamorous world of dollars and no sense. But reading a balance sheet was never my strong point. There were plenty of wonderful characters in those downtown canyons, but I never had time to write about them. I was too busy shopping. The death of my mother in 1979 woke me up to the fact that we don't live forever, so I decided to write or to forget my fantasy. My mother had always been my main cheerleader and champion. She glowed with pride when in Catholic grammar school I brought home my assignments, flowery paragraphs that I'd written about the Blessed Virgin on pages festooned with gold stars that I presented to mom in a never-ending bouquet. That's how I learned I could write. Ironically the subject I chose to write about would be the one topic she feared.

In the late 70's, early 80's the field of adult media offered a plethora of opportunities. It was just prior to the introduction of videocassettes that would put a serious dent in the production of all films, not just hardcore movies. America still rode the wave of sexual freedom that was ushered in by the invention of the birth control pill. Perhaps, most important, AIDS had not yet invaded the public consciousness. Condoms were old-fashioned. Sex was still very wet. This was the era of Plato's Retreat, the on-premise sex club that became the go-to destination for suburbanites and sophisticates. There were back room bars where gay men swapped fluids and connected through glory holes. Sadists and masochists congregated in well-equipped dungeons, the most notorious titled, ominously, Hellfire. New York was a wild west of sex. The hardcore film industry had not yet relocated to California. Hardcore producers still shot in town. Men's magazine publishers gave plenty of work to freelance writers and artists. A large industry attracts all kinds of people for all kinds of reasons.

The only person I knew who was making her living in the field of publishing was Mam'selle Victoire, the nom de plume of an aspiring actress from the Midwest. Her career detour took her to the offices of Bob Guccione's Penthouse Publications, where she helmed Variations, the magazine dedicated to alternative lifestyles for adventuresome couples, armchair voyeurs with an interest in swinging and kink. I met Mam'selle at the home of an art collector who liked to host musical salons he hoped would lead to sex. Mam'selle and I had partied together, sharing intimate moments while listening to Bach.

Forget the stereotypes, I wasn't a naive young girl, manipulated by some fat, sleazy cigar-chomper. I was a young woman of thirty, eager to explore my sexuality. From the beginning, I found camaraderie with women. They were my new madonnas, my shady madonnas. Mam'selle Victoire was the first. True to her name, she dressed as a woman from the 1890's, wearing skirts that brushed the floor, a tightly laced corset and her red hair worn like a crown in a Gibson girl 'do. I wrote and sold my first story to *Variations*. It was called *The Taste of Love*, about a man's first experiences with oral sex. I based the characters on the men I knew in Wall Street. I wrote under a male pseudonym, Anthony Vincent. I was now a published writer, but more than that a new door had opened and through it I met not only Mam'selle, but a host of other sexual explorers. Many of them were motivated not by money but by idealism, the desire to make the world a more sexually liberated place and to have a lot of fun doing it. That's when I met Annie Sprinkle.

Annie was riding high from the success of *Deep Inside Annie Sprinkle,* the movie that was the jewel in the crown of the multi-talented "golden girl of porn." Everything about her was unique. She had the look of a pirate: bracelets tattooed on her right arm, a diamond in her front tooth and full flowing mane of red hair. At five-foot-six, she was only about an inch taller than me, but she was statuesque. Her legs were long and lovely and usually encased in springolator mules with wooden platforms and skinny silver metal heels. The shoes came from the Paradise Bootery, a shoe store for strippers and hookers in a Times Square that no longer exists today. She was full busted, a DD cup, that usually spilled over the top of a

Jezebel bra and seemed even larger when she was squeezed into a corset. Bosom, boobs, bazoombas—she called them by different names and they were her breast assets (ouch).

From the moment we met, we became best friends. In her I recognized a dedicated pornographer. She was an outlaw, yet she remained sweet and innocent. Annie was an exhibitionist, yet also excruciatingly shy. She always referred to me as classy. After my years in the world of finance, I felt at ease in conversation with just about anyone. We complemented each other. I think she loved the fact that I had left the straight world, a world that she never felt comfortable in, and embraced hers. We were Lucy and Ethel, Thelma and Louise, Woodhull and Claflin. We were Annie and Veronica.

Annie lived in a spacious one bedroom apartment in a concierge building at 90 Lexington Avenue. The door to the apartment held a tiny sign that read, "Celebrate everything." The living room walls were pink and sprinkled with glitter. There was a collage of photos, pictures of her parents, her brothers and sister, interspersed with her friends and heroes: Fakir Musafar hanging in the sundance ritual with giant hooks in his chest, and Ethel Granger who measured 36-13-39 and achieved the smallest waist in the world. The wall just outside the kitchen was covered with framed 8 x 10 black-and-white glossies of Annie's porn star friends: Mark "10 1/2" Stevens, Gloria Leonard, Veronica Hart, Candida Royalle, Vanessa Del Rio, Jamie Gillis, Samantha Fox, Marleen Willoughby, and director Gerard Damiano were but a few. Her prettiest retro dresses, the sparkly green sequined sheath, the pink lace tea dress—all thrift shop finds—hung on the bedroom walls like great works for art. For Annie, the bedroom served as a closet. She preferred to sleep under a velvet and satin quilt on a futon in a corner of the living room. A little altar that held candles and flowers was right beside her head. The private bedroom was always available for out of town guests.

Annie loved being a hostess, a catalyst who could bring people and ideas together. I dubbed her apartment The Sprinkle Salon. Everywhere you looked there was something to see. Annie made it all available. She gave you her world.

I had dropped by the Sprinkle Salon for what I had planned as a quick visit, when Annie said, "Why don't you stay? Gerry Damiano will be here any minute to discuss my movie idea."

She had told me about this movie idea (There wasn't much that we didn't talk about).

"We'll go back to the 'weekend wonder'! Get lots of sexy people together for a couple of days and film whatever happens."

Though I already had performances in two videotapes under my garter belt, I had yet to perform hardcore sex in a movie or even get naked. With friends I'd met through Annie, Mistress Antoinette and Master Zorro, I'd made two videotapes, *Lisa's Rubber Seduction* and *Rebecca's Dream*. I was "Lisa," the rubber maid who got caught shimmying into her mistress's latex wardrobe. Rebecca's Dream showed me whipping the butt of the tightly corseted Rebecca H. Heels, a flamboyant transvestite who padded his triple E bra with a Nerf football. Unlike hardcore films with their close-up gynecological shots, these kinky videos were all about costumes. Some outfits were very elaborate, others not so. My co-star in *Lisa* got the biggest thrill when I wore an old-fashioned bathing cap with a chin strap. Making the movies was fun, but I was a writer. I planned to keep my clothes on, my legs together, and my porn cherry intact.

"Oh, stay," coaxed Annie, "I'll make us a nice pot of tea."

It was a brew like the bottle that Alice finds that says,

"Drink me." Annie never attributed any magical qualities to her tea, but things just sort of happened... Tea, well that sounded innocent enough. But tea with Mr. "Deep Throat" Damiano, the world's most infamous adult movie director? You didn't have to know anything about pornography to have heard of him. *Deep Throat* was the movie that initiated porno chic. Government prosecutions in the late 70's had paid off in instant notoriety for *Deep Throat* and college kids on campuses across the country stood in line to watch Linda Lovelace perform every man's fantasy, and certainly Gerry's. Like most auteurs, Gerry was an artist pursing his dream. Gerry's dream just happened to be blow jobs. *Deep Throat* is about a woman whose clitoris is located in her throat. Thus, giving head to others gives her immense pleasure. *Deep Throat* became the ultimate Saturday night date. And the government got involved.

The government crack-down on X-rated media, in particular, *Deep Throat*, brought with it another bonus for Gerry. He discovered Annie Sprinkle—at a trial in Tucson where she was called to testify because she was the popcorn girl in the theater that featured his movie. They became lovers, Gerry brought Annie to New York and, soon after, her career in front of the camera began. No longer lovers, they were now good friends, respected business associates. When one beckoned, the other came.

How could I resist the chance to meet Gerry? Would he be horned with a tail? Would he flash a fat wad of cash and have bodyguards or would he travel with a harem of sword-swallowers in mini-skirts? Being a Scorpio, I'm a born investigator. Meeting Gerry was research I couldn't resist.

From under a shock of white hair, a pearly smile spread across suntanned flesh. At once, he looked all soft and cuddly in a gold velour warm-up suit, more grandfather than godfather. He was also the golden guinea in his golden fleece who could play both god and the devil, and cast himself that way. His new wife was much younger and a vegetarian. I think he planned on living a long time. He wore a gold chain but no pinky ring. I was cautious, but curious.

The movie would be titled *Consenting Adults*, a quasi-documentary in which everyone played themselves. After some discussion, we decided that I would costar with Annie, but I was not going to perform sex in the movie. I had been interviewing people as a sex journalist for articles in a few men's magazines. In the movie, I would do the same thing, just on camera. Oh, I'd also flash my new acquisition, a gold nipple ring. Annie and I joked that I might become the only porn star who never got fucked on camera. That sounded okay to me. I liked being a "star," but the porn part, the sex part scared the hell out of me. I couldn't imagine spreading my legs for the camera. Art model was one thing. The pictures were tasteful and black-and-white. Porn requirements were more gynecological. I could not imagine exposing the juicy red flesh of my furry pussy. At the time, I was just getting used to seeing her myself, lovely though she was, a lush black orchid with full dark petals and a bright rosy center. I certainly wasn't ready to bare myself to the world in a way that could haunt me forever.

From the time so long ago when I reached into my cotton underpants, felt those first moments of heavenly bliss, only to be slapped when my mother scolded, "God does not like that" —God and my sexuality were linked. One part of me knew her words didn't ring true. The other part of me feared not just the loss of heaven, but the loss of my core, everything my mother and father had instilled in me about good and bad, and worse, the loss of that feeling of love. I knew I was playing with fire. No, I was not going to perform sex in that movie.

No worries, we had a very large cast of sexual enthusiasts. Day rates for performers in the early 80's was approximately $300-$500/day. Gerry was also producing this movie and like most producers, he was real good at crying poverty. Rumor had it that "Da Boyz," the syndicate that controlled the distribution of porn movies had made Gerry an offer he couldn't refuse and relieved him of the responsibility of keeping track of the profits of *Deep Throat*, along with most of the cash (at least, what was left of it after our legal system got its share). Since everyone wanted to work with Gerry and with Annie, even the established actors agreed to a day rate of $200.

The weekend-wonder would be shot at the Sprinkle Salon. It was a short shooting schedule in those days when adult films enjoyed five days to two weeks of filming. But compared to the current video quickies, *Consenting Adults* was an epic. It was in this minor masterpiece that I made my debut. To be honest, there were two such moments. Let's call them, the foreplay and the clincher.

The first occurred when we were shooting a scene in which Mr. 10 1/2 sat in a chair and stroked himself while a couple lay on the bed next to him and made love. Marc "10 1/2" Stevens was a genius of self-promotion. The 10 1/2 referred not to his shoe size. I appreciated all 10 1/2 inches as I sat off camera in my lingerie and watched the action. He spread his legs and slouched back. His mouth dropped open slightly as he enjoyed this masturbation. Annie and I sat off to the side, our legs spread as we pleasured ourselves, eager voyeurs in lingerie. The scene went on and on and I watched fascinated, my eyes mostly on Marc and his proud, hard penis. I knew I was good at oral sex. I wanted to take him in my mouth. To look in his eyes and see that moment when he would feel my power as the warm, wetness enveloped him. The scene was almost over. A symphony of moans and groans and heavy breathing signaled its approaching climaxes. The cameras didn't frighten me. I planned to dash in and out almost before they saw and let my hair hide my face as my mouth opened on top of Marc. So I jumped in and dropped to my knees, eager to worship at the altar of phallus, eager to become part of this raunchy repertory, but anxious for him not to come in my face. No spunk on the eyelashes please. Up and down, up and down, and then back on my heels, leaving Marc plenty of room for the money shot. Each of two cameras captured each of two ejaculations and I made sure neither of them got a good look at sneaky little me. Not long after, I would be ready for my close-up.

"Clear the set."

On location in the parlor Gerry Damiano and the crew waited patiently as Annie Sprinkle attempted to re-enact a date with one of her lovers, Michael Cycle. The Cycle got his name because of the Harley usually parked between his thighs. He was a beautiful ape of a man: long, matted afro, muscles, tattoos. He slugged from a bottle of beer and tried to act cool and macho, but there was a problem with his penis. He'd never made an X-rated movie and the hot lights, the many watchful eyes, the pressure to perform hindered his dicktorial debut.

All of us not essential to the scene were herded into the bedroom. In one corner, a transsexual dominatrix gave her wimpy slave a whispered tongue-lashing. My dear friend Denis Florio, "picture framer to the stars," had been hired to guard the front door. He given himself the nom de porn Dino D'Macho and was busy in the closet playing hide the salami with the gay make-up man. I had helped Annie to put the film together: assembling the cast and crew, working out the scenes. I felt part of the inner circle, so I was not happy that the set was closed to me, too.

"Veronica," Annie's voice called to me from the living room.

Maybe she'd read the disappointment in my face as we were lead away, or maybe Annie reasoned that if I jumped into the scene with her and Michael Cycle, he would be so busy with two women on his hands, he would have no time to worry about his dick, and he'd get it up.

"Veronica…."

This was my moment of truth. If I was going to be a porn star, it was going to be now. I had to decide. But I hadn't dressed for the camera. I wore panty hose and no make-up. My legs were hairy, I was not prepared and I was SCARED. This was an act I could never take back. This would be recorded forever... my shame. What shame? I was sick of shame. I wanted to break through my fears.

"I want to... I want to..."

I ran from the bedroom and leaped onto the mattress. The Cycle pulled my dress over my head and ripped my pantyhose. His big rough hands reached between my legs to that core of pleasure I had discovered as a little girl in the center of my soft cotton underpants.

Annie lay spread eagle on her back, smiling into the camera.

"Veronica and I have never made love before. She's never put her finger inside of me or anything."

(Well, almost never.)

I wanted to make love to her. But did I want to do it in front of the camera?

I dove into Annie's big milky breast cushions, lost inside Mommy's nurturing breasts. I licked her nipples, her belly, her thighs. Her naked cunt glared at me like some hypnotic third eye, so delicate, so frightening, so powerful, so pink!

Behind me, Michael Cycle cooed romantically, "Lift your butt." His dick was hard and eager. He liked my wide ass. He urged his cock into the curves of my vagina, like he leaned his Harley into a tight mountain road. I lowered my tongue to take communion from the sacred hole of Annie Sprinkle and popped my porn cherry once and for all.

My eyes peered from above her close-cropped pubic hair. There was no room to hide. "Don't let me see the camera," I thought. "Don't let the camera see me. Don't let Mommy see me. Don't let Daddy see me. Don't let God see me... Let the whole world see me. I'm a fucking movie star!"

Afterward, I stood in front of the bathroom mirror and thought to myself, "Well, you're still here. God didn't strike you dead with a lightening bolt." On the contrary, I never felt more alive. I felt committed... to the film, yes, but more than that, I was committed to being me. That was just the beginning. I was free.

A Porn Star Remembers... Senator Arlen Specter

The long arms of our laws reach out to entire segments of the population. Occasionally, Washington has a need for more personal contact. We, as individuals, are plucked from our Lilliputian lives and offered the opportunity to bear witness to the truth as we know it.

In 1984, the U.S. government began hearings to determine if new laws were needed around the issue of pornography. Under particular scrutiny were the sexually explicit images of hardcore pornography. In Indianapolis, a federal judge contemplated legislation proposed by anti-porn feminists led by attorney Catherine Mackinnon and poet Andrea Dworkin, which would make pornography a violation of a woman's civil rights. A call went out for volunteers from both sides of the issue who would testify before a Committee of the Senate Judiciary, chaired by Senator Arlen Specter. Uncle Sam tapped me on the shoulder, crooked his little finger in my direction and summoned with a provocative come-hither look. I could have said, "No," but that wasn't my style.

My credentials as a witness were based on having performed in a half dozen sexually explicit movies—a mere drop in the bucket compared to the careers of most stars of the sex-splattered cinema. But I had not stopped there. Since 1979, I had played the lead in my own continuing movie—erotic model and performer, sex journalist-documenting each step of the way with words and images. My career had been extraordinary. I had managed to meet and collaborate with artists whose works would expand sexual and creative freedom for years to come. Annie Sprinkle, who would become the first porn star to gain a Ph.D., was reigning at the time as the queen of the golden shower and my best friend. Gerard Damiano whose *Deep Throat* had begun the era of porno chic that brought adult films to college campuses, directed me in my first movie. My collaborations with Robert Mapplethorpe resulted in his first heterosexual images of hardcore sex. These photos had graced the walls of the Whitney Museum. Conversely, in the interest of thoroughness and accurate reporting, I had also run into my fair share of hopeless reprobates and ventured into some of the sleaziest dives and diversions. The day that I met and testified before Senator Arlen Specter remains in my memory one of the most exciting and meaningful days of my extraordinary and totally unexpected career as a sexual evolutionary.

There was something very comforting about the Senate Gallery. A blond wooden dais arced the front of the room. It shone like a church pew polished lovingly by the backsides of the faithful. At the center of the dais sat Senator Arlen Specter. He was flanked wall to wall by thirty Senate aides—young men and women in crisp suits, a pen in each hand, a pad in each lap. I sat before them, legs crossed at the knees, hands folded on the desk. I wore a royal blue dress and around my neck was an amethyst necklace that had belonged to my mother. It was my amulet. In choosing to testify, I felt I represented not only myself, not simply other women, but many people of all genders who valued freedom of sexual expression. That kind of weight required broad shoulders. Good thing mine were padded.

Joining me at the witness desk was Seka, a true porn queen and "the blonde goddess." She had made her entrance in a fox fur, surrounded by an entourage of men in suits who carried attaché cases. In her testimony, she focused on herself as an "adult in the business of adult entertainment." Now it was my turn.

The introductory statement I prepared was a comparison of the myths and realities of porn as I experienced them. I began:

"Myth: women in porn have unhappy childhoods. Reality: I come from a very loving family. That core of love has always been my strength. I was raised as a Catholic and while I do not practice…"

My voice cracked, the words stopped, and were strangled in my throat as my subconscious felt the tug of my family's love and my early devotions. I was all choked up. And no one was more surprised than me. I had prepared my speech and was eager to be heard. The woman in me was ready, but the little girl who always tried to do everything right was frightened. Just saying the words, recalling my family, and the rich religion of my childhood, had brought up so much emotion that I had to stop.

The video I received later, showed that at this point, my long fingernails flashed bright red as I reached for a glass of water and resumed. "Excuse me Senator… I mean what I say." That sentence was superfluous. Senator Specter was a former District Attorney. I have no doubt he could tell when a witness before him revealed gut-wrenching truths.

At the conclusion of my prepared statement, the Senator questioned me. He held some photographs, which I had submitted for the edification of the committee. The Senator looked from me to the images. In one shot, I stood bound in rope, legs close together, wrists tight behind my back, giving me that phallic armless look. In another, I knelt, my back to the camera, casting a worried look over my shoulder, while flaunting my raised and oh, so vulnerable buttocks.

A series of photos showed my delicate pink panties sliced open with a scissors. My labia were spread by the fingers of our off-stage bondage consultant, my best friend and collaborator, the porn star Annie Sprinkle (always there for me in a pinch). She helped me to display my swollen clitoris and the entrance to my vagina.

It was the first time I'd ever shown pink in a magazine, and here it had made it all the way to Capitol Hill. God bless America.

Senator Specter began, "Ms. Vera, this publication which is captioned, 'Veronica Vera in Tight Bondage' is similar to others that have been brought to this committee by women who said they were fearful such publications would cause other women to be forced into these positions against their will. Do you think there is nothing to that kind of concern?"

"Against our will, Senator? Believe me, there are plenty of volunteers. Do you know that the New York Times quotes bondage as the number one fantasy among women and men?"

I thought, "Ban these photos, Senator, well then you'd better ban the Bible and the lives of The Saints, because that's what inspired me."

I told the Senator that my purpose in posing for the photos was to explore my own bondage fantasies and to learn from them. I asked him if I might read a paragraph I wrote that accompanied the photos and he said, yes.

Except for one woman in the back who thumped her bible and chanted, "Jesus, Jesus, Jesus," the room was a total hush. The audience hung on my every word as I read, "I am the love toy, the object of your desire, exposed and vulnerable. Picture yourself tying the ropes, keeping me as your captive, ready to be taken whenever you want me. Always open to your..."

The next words flashed before me like red lights at a railroad crossing. Television cameras were all around, and my mind reeled as I tried to recall the seven "dirty" words forbidden by the FCC. "Shit, piss, tits, cunt, fuck, cocksucker, motherfucker..."

Senator Specter had the same text in front of him. I decided to let him give me the signal. "Shall I go on, Senator?"

His answer rang out loud and clear, resounding in my ear like the clang of the Liberty Bell.

"You certainly may."

Gleefully, I continued: "Always open to your cock and

your mouth. Enjoy me, take pleasure from me. When you do, you will understand. Through the purity of my surrender, you have become my captive, too." Emboldened, I addressed him, "Senator Specter, I don't want to be a victim. I don't want to be considered a victim. I think we need to be free to explore our fantasies."

"It is depicted that you are being squeezed, tied in a variety of positions, really, as you say, very vulnerable, very much exposed…"

My mind filled with the images and experiences that fueled my fantasies and were the prequels to those glossy pages. I thought, "Yes, yes, go on Senator, tell me what you see. Do you see the whore who wants to be punished? Do you see the cowgirl tied up by the Indians? Do you see the martyr about to have her nipples chopped? Do you see the woman trussed up and ridiculous? Do you see the sex goddess, the fertility symbol? Do you see the bitch in heat who yearns to be touched? Do you see the little girl who discovered pleasure in the center of her soft cotton underpants? Can you understand that what you see is not simple? Do you understand that all of these women are me?"

I'd done a symbolic striptease and bared my soul. It was so much more of a challenge than baring my breasts. The hearing continued. At its conclusion, Senator Specter walked over to thank me for my testimony. He shook my hand. Firmly. In that handshake, I felt him reach across the years. It was my right hand, the hand that had found its way to that font of pleasure so long ago. It was the hand with which I touched myself, the hand that led me astray, and the hand that would always bring me home.

The Senator bore witness to my outrageous testimony and accepted it without passing judgment. The government touched me in the person of Senator Arlen Spector and I returned its grip. The acknowledgement in the form of that handshake gave me faith in the Democratic process and bolstered my faith in myself, and my experiences as a woman and as a citizen. I had been heard. I made contact. Thank you, Senator Arlen Spector. Rest in peace.

Note: The legislation that was contemplated in Indianapolis was eventually struck down. The hearing in which I testified was later incorporated into the Report of the Commission created in 1985 by then Attorney General Edwin Meese. By its end The Meese Report, as it became know, would examine 2375 magazines, 725 books and 2370 movies.

Veronica Vera chronicled her own sex life and that of New York as a journalist throughout the 1980's, the decade in which she was a porn star, erotic mode and activist. At the start of the 90's, she began work on a memoir about what she had learned. At the same time, she began to help men in their own processes of female liberation and instead of just a sideline this work, made transgender history when she founded the world's first crossdressing academy, Miss Vera's Finishing School for Boys who Want to Be Girls and authored two books about her school. Now it is time to finish that original memoir and treat others to a time that will and should never be forgotten, a time when sex was fun and sex was wet, and porn was filled with artists and idealists. Veronica thanks Red Umbrella Project for help in this project. In June 2012, Veronica Vera married Stuart Ira Cottingham. They live happily in NYC. www.missvera.com

Acknowledgements

The Red Umbrella Project would like to thank the New York Women's Foundation for the generous funding that made The Becoming Writers Workshop, this book, and many of our other 2012 and 2013 programs possible. We are also grateful to Poets & Writers and the New York State Council of the Arts for additional funding that supported the workshop and Red Umbrella Diaries events celebrating the writers.

Additional thank you's must be extended to Tamara Oyola-Santiago and the New School for hosting our classes, Sayaka Isowa for the gorgeous cover art, and Olivia Hall for designing the book.

About the Editor

Melissa Petro is a freelance writer and teacher. Her writing has appeared in has appeared on *Salon, Daily Beast, The Huffington Post, Guardian, Jezebel, Bitch Magazine* and *elsewhere*. The story documenting the experience of her losing her job as a public elementary school teacher after writing about her sex work past was one of *Salon's* 100 most trafficked stories of 2011. She holds a Masters degree in Creative Nonfiction from the New School.

About Red Umbrella Project

The Red Umbrella Project (RedUP) amplifies the voices of people who have done transactional sex, through media, storytelling, and advocacy programs. We are a small and feisty New York-based organization that is run by and for our community of people who trade sex for things they need. We offer workshops in media, advocacy, writing, and storytelling for people in the sex industry, and collaborate on community organizing projects in New York and beyond. We also produce a monthly live storytelling series, the Red Umbrella Diaries, where people in the sex trades share true stories about their lives in front of a public audience. We record everyone who wishes their story to be documented and have published more than seventy episodes on our Red Umbrella Diaries podcast, which is available for free on iTunes. Learn more at http://redumbrellaproject.org and http://redumbrelladiaries.com.

Printed in Poland
by Amazon Fulfillment
Poland Sp. z o.o., Wrocław